The Sobriety Secret:  an

By Craig Beck

Copyright Stop Drinking Expert

This book reflects the personal experience of the author. It is not intended as a substitute for professional assistance but describes a program to be undertaken only under the supervision of a medical doctor or other qualified healthcare professional. Individual results may vary.

Want to make this easy? Find out more about the world's most successful and respected quit drinking course here: https://www.stopdrinkingexpert.com/

THE SOBRIETY SECRET: WHY QUITTING DRINKING IS EASIER THAN YOU THINK   1

Introduction	4
Chapter 1: It Starts With A First Step	6
Chapter 2: Step Away From The Mousetrap!	27
Chapter 3: The Illusion Of The Evil Clown?	46
Chapter 4: The Stupid Genius	60
Chapter 5: Alcohol And Mental Health	68
Chapter 6: Alcohol – The Wolf Is In The Camp	74
Chapter 7: Antonis's Trip To Hell	81
Chapter 8: Lie Down with Dogs – Get Up with Fleas	90
Chapter 9: Threshold	102
Chapter 10: Deconstructing the Addiction	113
Chapter 11: Balance, Not Battle	123
Chapter 12: Expensive Poison	131
Chapter 13: A Little External Help	138
Omega-3 Capsules (1000 mg)	140
B Vitamin Complex	141
Vitamin D	141
Magnesium	142
Curcumin	142
Chapter 14: Controlling the Evil Clown	149
Chapter 15: Dealing With the Kick	160

Chapter 16: Questions! 167

Chapter 17: The Complete Solution 183

Online Course 190

Introduction

Picture a life where every morning begins without a pounding head and a ransacked wallet—where your energy isn't siphoned off by shame or an endless cycle of "just one more." This is precisely what The Sobriety Secret aims to deliver. Building on the success of Alcohol Lied To Me, Craig Beck presents a fresh approach to transforming your relationship with alcohol. The Sobriety Secret weaves together proven principles from NLP psychology, the real-life triumphs and stumbles of someone who's wrestled with addiction, and the practiced wisdom of a qualified therapist, personal coach, and bestselling quit lit author. Rather than offering a string of empty prompts, this resource carefully choreographs each day's reflection, drawing you toward a richer, more authentic way of living without the familiar shadow of a hangover.

It's designed to help you seize every last benefit that sobriety parades in front of you. Money is often the first revelation: by tracking the financial black hole of your drinking, you may be shoccked to discover the small fortune once poured away at bars and social gatherings. Yet cash is only one reward. A deeper sense of well-being surfaces when you stop punishing your body for some fleeting buzz and instead explore how your thoughts, moods, and physical health connect. Each reflection invites you to gauge your emotional triggers—be they certain environments, specific people, or random events that twist your arm toward picking up a drink. You even have space to scribble down resentments that bubble up, because sometimes newly sober folks find they briefly hate everything that breathes. It's quite normal, and acknowledging it can open a door to genuine healing.

Then there's the reassuring knowledge that you're part of a community who understand every slip, every proud milestone, and every tearful confession. Having tamed their own cravings, these individuals can offer real empathy when your optimism wavers or your mind concocts excuses for "just a sip." In short, The Sobriety Secret envelops you in practical strategies, emotional support, and a meticulously structured daily routine that gently steers you toward an empowering, hangover-free existence. If you commit to it, you'll discover what countless others have: sobriety can be the catalyst for more time, vitality, and adventure than you ever imagined.

www.stopdrinkingexpert.com

Chapter 1: It Starts With A First Step

It often begins with a quiet, nagging sense of dissonance. You notice a thought creeping around the edges of your mind, whispering that there's something off about the way your using alcohol—some elusive itch that refuses to go away. Perhaps the realization starts with a small, unsettling moment, like catching a glimpse of the recycling bin overflowing with empty bottles, or maybe it's the awkward memory of a night when the bedroom spinning felt a bit too relentless. Nothing earth-shattering, just a faint internal voice muttering, "This isn't quite right, is it?"

That's the early seed of doubt. People often push it away: "Everyone drinks," or "I'm just going through a phase," or "Work's been tough—this is how I manage stress." Yet the niggling question resurfaces whenever there's a lull in the day. It's the quiet in-between times—driving to work, waiting in line, or lying in bed wide awake at 2:00 a.m.—when the beliefs start to fray, and reality sneaks in. Over time, these small warnings add up, but folks still hold tight to social proof, reminding themselves that normal people also love a glass or two. The idea that their drinking might be a problem can feel too large, too cumbersome to handle. So they bury it, hoping that if they don't disturb it, it'll simply vanish.

Of course, it doesn't vanish. Instead, the doubts accumulate, like a collection of sticky notes pinned to a bulletin board. Maybe you told yourself you'd only drink on weekends, but you find yourself opening a bottle of wine on a Wednesday evening. Maybe you vowed to never again show up hungover for the kids' soccer game, then promptly woke up on the couch the next day with a splitting headache. Each broken promise is like another neon sign blinking in your periphery, even if you pretend not to notice.

Over months or years, life can start to feel subtly smaller. There might be intangible costs—lost energy, creeping shame, arguments that spark out of nowhere. The spouse or partner mentions your drinking in a concerned tone, which triggers a defensive response. Friends invite you out, and you weigh the importance of the event against the chance to stay home and drink in your usual, self-controlled environment. Perhaps you used to relish trying new hobbies or traveling spontaneously, but now everything revolves around maintaining access to your beverage of choice. This process can be so incremental you barely see it happening. You think, "I'm still successful. I still have my job." But you feel the creep of emptiness behind the daily routines.

Eventually, a sharper jolt tends to arrive. It might be embarrassment at a work function where you said something you regret, your memory hazy the next morning. Or a doctor's appointment where you're told your blood pressure looks problematic, prompting the doc to raise an eyebrow about your drinking habits. Sometimes it's a financial wake-up call when you realize how much you've spent on fancy bottles or bar tabs. Or maybe you see your child's expression as they quietly register your slump on the sofa yet again. These moments rattle your beliefs, like a hammer cracking a delicate shell. It's not necessarily an utter meltdown—no job lost, no extreme meltdown at a family wedding—but it's enough to stir real worry. You can't bury the question anymore.

Still, many continue to cling to false beliefs. The brain tries to rationalize: "It's not that big a deal. I can handle it." But now there's a tension in the back of the mind, a sense that if you carry on ignoring it, you're risking bigger consequences down the road. You have episodes of mild dread. Waking up at 3:00 a.m. with a pounding heart, you replay last night's conversation or that silly text you sent, and the ball of anxiety in your stomach grows. This typically is the phase where people begin considering searching for a label to explain their behavior—wondering if they're borderline "alcoholic" or if it's simply stress. Yet the stigma of that word can make them squeamish. They prefer to say "I might be drinking a bit too much these days," never referencing the big A-word.

So what triggers them to type something into Google about their relationship with alcohol? Usually, a convergence of factors that build a sense of urgency. Maybe a friend confesses they're cutting back, and it sparks jealousy or confusion. Or they read an article about the rise of "mommy wine culture," and for an instant, they see themselves in it. Possibly they read an obituary of a public figure who died from liver complications or see a documentary about addiction. That's all it can take to push them over the threshold. The lies are wearing thin, so they think, "I'll just do a quick check online. I'm sure I'm fine, but let me just see what the experts say about recommended drinking guidelines."

They open a browser late at night. The house is quiet, the usual glass half-finished on the coffee table. The keyboard beckons, and they type in queries like "Am I drinking too much?" or "Signs I'm dependent on alcohol." There's a strange knot in their stomach because part of them doesn't want to see the answers. But a bigger part realizes they're done burying that nagging voice.

The first pages that pop up can be enlightening. They see checklists: "Have you ever lied to a friend about how much you drank?" "Have you tried to stop and failed?" "Do you find yourself obsessing over the next opportunity for a drink?" This triggers a sudden flush of recognition. Some of those bullet points land dangerously close to home. Perhaps they see personal stories of professionals who struggled in silence. Maybe they read about moderate drinkers who gradually slid into daily use. They notice how many paragraphs describe experiences eerily similar to their own. Now the lies are cracking. Reading about real people who overcame the habit can spark both relief and alarm—relief that it's not just them, alarm that they might be deeper in than they realized.

Their next move might be more searching. "How do I stop drinking on my own?" "Is there a way to cut back safely?" "Tips for coping with cravings." They open multiple tabs, scanning stories, medical advice, articles from rehab centers. The fact that they're doing this often late at night adds to the sense of secrecy, a mild shame about even needing these resources. Yet searching signals a shift. They're no longer solely reliant on old beliefs. Something new is stirring.

There's a vulnerability in that moment. If they stumble on a site that says, "It's no big deal, keep going," they might cling to that for comfort. But typically, they're confronted with consistent facts: Drinking is associated with more damage than they dared suspect. It's linked to heartbreak, health crises, and financial strain. They see themselves in the stories. They see advice about seeing a doctor, exploring therapy, or picking up a book about how to break free. That's when they might think, "Alright, I'll order a self-help guide—just to see if it resonates."

By the time they place an online order for a quit-drinking resource, they've admitted to themselves, at least in part, that they aren't content continuing as they are. They might not be fully ready to say, "I have a problem," but they sense the slope is steep, and they've begun sliding. And all the old porgramming, like "I just enjoy the taste," or "Everyone else does it," or "I can stop whenever I want," are wavering under the weight of real evidence. That mental pivot can take months or even years to arrive, but once it's there, the search for solutions becomes unstoppable.

Right at the outset, I want to tackle the question that nags at so many: do you actually have a problem with alcohol? The truth is that anyone who consumes this drug in any dose or frequency is inviting trouble. There is no getting around that. The idea that someone can participate in this chemical habit without consequences is built on smoke and mirrors: alcohol is pure toxin, sold in glittering bottles, advertised with huge budgets, and so entwined with culture that most folks can no longer separate reality from clever marketing.

Try pointing out to your drinking buddies that they're essentially ingesting poison, and watch the emotional fireworks. People do not like having their sacred cows criticized, especially when it involves the beverage they believe is harmless or even beneficial. They'll insist that millions of normal people worldwide drink responsibly. They'll claim that a small portion of the population might have problems, but certainly not them. They'll even argue that a casual drink can enhance life in certain scenarios—like a romantic dinner or a celebratory toast. Yet all those counterarguments rely on turning a blind eye to the most important fact: you're ingesting a registered poison born from decaying vegetable matter. It's bizarre, if you think about it, that many of us have been convinced this is a perfectly normal activity.

Imagine, for argument's sake, that instead of wine or vodka, we were dealing with little vials of cyanide. It's the same kind of lethal agent—just a different label. Would you describe a person who occasionally downs a few drops of cyanide as a "social user"? The concept is absurd, obviously. But that's precisely what we do with alcohol. People might say, "But pure cyanide will kill you instantly, whereas alcohol just makes you feel a bit tipsy." Sure, pure alcohol would also kill you right away if you drank enough of it. Diluted cyanide might merely make you violently sick, in much the same way that diluted alcohol leads to hangovers and organ damage. We're not exactly comparing apples with oranges.

Once you accept that this drug is lethal at heart, it becomes possible to see beyond all the illusions. Suddenly, the phrases "social drinker" or "responsible drinker" reveal themselves as meaningless. They are daydreams that keep us from acknowledging that addiction doesn't come with big neon signs. The so-called "functional" alcoholic might once have been a part of that pool of casual sippers everyone calls normal. It's only later, when the invisible trap has snapped shut, that society bestows them with the pitiful label "alcoholic." Now they're ridiculed for failing to master a drug that was never safe in the first place. Indeed, marketing campaigns have spent generations weaving stories about how sexy and sophisticated you become once you fill your glass. Where's the glamour in reeking of booze and telling the same slurred joke for the tenth time in a night?

We talk about having a night on the town and then brag the next morning that we were "hammered," "smashed," or "absolutely slaughtered"—terms that evoke violence or destruction—yet we utter them like badges of honor. The way we celebrate negative words as if they're positive achievements speaks to the giant mind trick that alcohol has managed to pull on billions of people. Meanwhile, the reality is far less glossy: watch a tipsy stranger try to flirt when you're sober. Nothing sexy about that, is there? The unfortunate soul can barely keep from drooling or repeating themselves, let alone exude effortless charm.

This cultural double standard was hammered into my own head for years. I, too, believed that certain forms of alcohol, the ones that came in fancy bottles and cost a small fortune, offered a refined pleasure. I had visions of swirling, sniffing, and analyzing an expensive Bordeaux as though I were sipping the nectar of the gods. If the label bragged about how it was stored in oak casks in some mystical region of France, I'd nod sagely, as though that explained the wine's "bold character." In truth, it was still the same chemical compound that leaves your brain battered and your wallet emptier. Maybe I spent five hundred dollars on a bottle, but it was still an addictive compound. The prettiest packaging doesn't change its fundamental nature.

The lies I piled on myself were borderline comic. I had a wine cellar at home—temperature-controlled, filled with a variety of so-called artisanal wines. My children would be told to leave me in peace after a tough day, so I could "relax" with my beloved bottles. I'd swirl the liquid in a crystal glass, pausing to admire the color in the light, inhaling the heady aroma, feeling so very superior. I'd pat myself on the back for possessing such refined taste, even as I was spending money we didn't really have. The fact that my children were losing out on a family trip that year, while my cellar was well-stocked, highlighted just how delusional I had become.

Looking back, it's painfully obvious that my elaborate rituals were no more elevated than a homeless person's paper-bagged whiskey. It was the same chemical. It was the same addictive lure. I just decorated it with a big fat "expert connoisseur" label so that, psychologically, I could pretend I was miles above the person drinking out of a plastic cup. My delusions ran so deep that on nights out, if a waiter or sommelier recognized me and offered me premium service and a seat of honor, I'd beam like a child receiving candy. I thought it made me special, deserving of admiration, and that it proved I was living a glamorous life. My wife at the time, who was forced to watch me ignore her for half the evening while I sniffed and slurped the next expensive sample, had a completely different perspective. She saw an ego-fueled fool letting a random stranger hijack a date night, while the server practically drooled at the possibility of selling me a bottle that cost more than our kids' new shoes. An addictive toxin didn't addle her memory, so she could see reality far more clearly than I could.

Yet society props up these lies with gusto. The entire industry is built on them. We cling to ideas that good wine or craft beer is an indulgence that shows off our refined palate. We don't want to see the illogical core of it all. The doctors won't be rummaging around in your insides one day, congratulating you for having a classy brand in your liver. Alcohol is a single chemical, and it does the same damage no matter what it costs or how fancy the label. The delusion that somehow we're "above" problem drinking if our wine is expensive or our whiskey is single malt is just plain nonsense.

The World Health Organization does not mince words when describing alcohol's global toll. They don't differentiate cheap wine from premium scotch. They talk about the high volume of deaths and the litany of social, developmental, and familial harms. They point out that this one drug is responsible for so much lost potential, so many destroyed relationships, so much physical and psychological damage. Very few people like to think about that when they pop the cork at a party, but it's the inconvenient truth that never goes away.

Sometimes people protest, "But what about the difference between a homeless guy slugging grocery-store whiskey on the curb and a wealthy professional who sips a 1982 Bordeaux with dinner?" The difference is mostly cosmetic. The biggest variation might just be in how quickly or visibly the damage accumulates. The poor soul on the park bench might get labeled a hopeless case faster because it's out in the open. The white-collar drinker, by contrast, could carry on for years as a so-called "functional" alcoholic. But functional or not, eventually the damage creeps in, physically, mentally, or socially. It's just a matter of time.

Some folks cling to the excuse that they don't smoke, as if that proves they're not actually that bad. The logic usually goes, "Well, I could be doing worse. Cigarettes are lethal, so at least I'm only indulging in a drink now and then." But the statistics often show that for certain demographics—particularly middle earners—alcohol is actually a more serious killer. And while the smokers among us have to endure increasingly restrictive smoking bans and harsh societal judgment, drinkers are still widely celebrated. It's a deeply ingrained hypocrisy that encourages us to keep the blindfold on a little longer.

Alcohol is known as the silent killer precisely because it slides under your radar. There's rarely that loud internal alarm going off until it's far too late. The casual user imagines they'll see the warning signs if they ever start to lose control, but that's just another miscalculation. The cunning part is that by the time you realize you might be in trouble, you're usually already halfway to the bottom of a pit. The organ that suffers the most under heavy use is the liver, which is terrifyingly resilient and has almost no nerve endings. It'll keep you going, quietly repairing itself, until the damage is so severe that you suddenly experience intense pain or other dramatic symptoms. By then, you're often in deep trouble. And if you think a liver transplant is your fallback plan, you may be in for a rude awakening when you find yourself behind thousands of other desperately ill people on a waiting list.

No one wakes up one morning with a neon sign blinking over their head proclaiming "Alcoholic!" The shift from "social drinking" to "dependence" can be eerily gradual, sneaking up on you like an unexpected thief in the night. We'd all like to believe we're immune or that "it won't happen to me," but the trap is set the moment you start using an addictive substance regularly. It's entirely possible some people can go for years without consequences, but that doesn't negate the fundamental risk. It's like carrying around a grenade in your pocket and betting it never goes off.

We draw all sorts of distinctions between moderate drinkers and the more extreme daily users. The latter get slapped with the label "alcoholic" and told they have an incurable disease, often being directed to identify themselves by that grim word for the rest of their lives. They attend group meetings, recite confessions, and attempt to rely on willpower to avoid the bar or the liquor aisle. It's no wonder a massive percentage give up and return to drinking. The approach is self-punishing. It insists you're broken, and the best you can do is keep fighting day after day until your dying breath.

Alcoholics Anonymous has helped some people—there's no question about that. But it's less than ideal for the majority, partly because it relies on the concept of willpower to remain abstinent. Willpower can move mountains in certain areas of life, but relying on it to overcome an addiction can be like trying to hold your breath underwater indefinitely. Eventually, you need to breathe. If you regard alcohol as something you still want but must heroically resist, you're forever living with tension. It's exhausting and tends to end in relapse for most.

It's like juggling flaming torches. Sooner or later, you're going to get burned. The difference is we wouldn't label you "fireaholic" if you got hurt. We'd just note that playing with fire is dangerous in almost any context, so maybe you should keep your distance from those flames. With alcohol, we label the user the problem rather than the substance, turning it into a moral failing or a disease. So the poor individual is saddled with shame, while the real culprit—the toxic chemical—remains glorified.

You're not an "alcoholic." You're a human being who stumbled into a trap set by a substance that is inherently addictive. If 80% of Western society drinks, and a huge chunk of them become dependent, that's hardly a sign that this drug is harmless. It's more an indication that we've normalized a harmful behavior on a massive scale. Commercials show parties in full swing and always highlight the brand that supposedly "makes the night." Meanwhile, behind the scenes, alcohol stands as one of the most nefarious and cunning killers known to humanity.

Maybe you're reading this and nodding, but there's still that stubborn voice in your head protesting, "Yeah, but I'm different. I don't have a problem. My life is under control. Sure, I enjoy a drink, but that doesn't mean I'm an alcoholic." My guess is that people close to you have raised a few eyebrows about your habits, or you wouldn't be here. The very fact you're looking for clarity suggests you already sense something is amiss. Perhaps you're searching for confirmation you can keep going as you are, or maybe you're daring yourself to see how bad it's become. Either way, these pages won't sugarcoat it.

If any of the following ring a bell—like planning your schedule around when you can drink, or telling yourself you'll only drink beer instead of spirits, or hearing concerned friends mention your consumption—then you've already drifted into dangerous territory. If you've tried to cut down or quit before and fallen back to old habits, that's an even clearer signal. I deliberately avoid labeling you an "alcoholic" because I know how quickly that term triggers defensiveness. People will exclaim, "I drink too much sometimes, but I'm not an alcoholic!" The stigma is huge. I remember I refused to consider myself an alcoholic when I was polishing off vast amounts nightly, because that would mean I was a "weak," "pathetic" person. In reality, I was just another regular individual who got caught in the powerful suction of a drug sold on nearly every corner.

This is the real mind-bending twist: many people who meet official criteria for dependence still manage to hold down their jobs, maintain a family, and keep up appearances. They're the so-called functional alcoholics. They show up to the office on time, maybe with a mild hangover, but they're charismatic enough that folks rarely guess how bad it is behind the scenes. Some are so adept at juggling that no one suspects a thing. They might excel in high-profile careers and appear outwardly successful, but inside, they're living in a private prison they can't seem to escape.

I was one of those folks—marching into a broadcasting job each day, well-groomed and outwardly confident, while quietly planning how I'd get home as soon as possible to uncork a bottle. If that is your situation, you're not alone. You're walking a path shared by countless others who've discovered how easy it is for an occasional glass to become a must-have comfort blanket. Worse yet, society is all too willing to keep the secret for you because it's awkward to question someone's drinking, especially if they appear to be functioning just fine.

But it catches up. Alcohol has a way of dragging you into a swirling loop of misery if you ignore the signs. You run faster and faster, but you remain stuck in place. The scenic background never changes, like you're living in some kind of animated cartoon. This is the place where self-pity can flourish. You might start adopting the idea that you suffer from an incurable "disease" called alcoholism, as if you stumbled into it by random chance, so how could you possibly be blamed?

Yet this stance helps no one. Even if you read all the psychology textbooks in the world or gather the best family history arguments to rationalize your predicament, you're still pouring a potent chemical down your throat every time you drink. I've worked with many people who've spent more time researching the background causes of addiction than actually doing anything about their own daily routine. Once you step into that blame game—blaming your parents, your genetics, a stressful job, or the advertisements that plaster your local bus stop—you've essentially surrendered your power to fix the situation.

In my stop drinking program, for instance, you'd quickly find out that I'm not the coddling kind of mentor who strokes your hair and says how unfortunate you are. This drug is nasty, but it's also cunning, and the delusions propping it up are deeply entrenched. If you're serious about ditching it, there's no room for the pity party. It's natural to feel some despair or frustration along the way, but it's action and understanding that lay the pathway out of this addictive maze.

Inside the members' area of that program, it's fascinating to see the polar opposites: people who've been sober for half a decade, living vibrant lives, and individuals who still spiral back into daily drinking after only a few attempts at abstinence. What's the key difference? From where I stand, it's that the sober ones are prepared to do what the active drinkers won't. They toss aside their excuses—those pre-loaded reasons for delaying the day of reckoning—and they step up, acknowledging that their own determination is not optional. In contrast, the ones who remain stuck often have an unending list of "tomorrow" reasons. "Work is crazy right now," "I'll quit after the holidays," "I deserve a break after all I've been through." The wheel keeps turning, and the bar tab keeps climbing.

When you cut out all that noise, your path to freedom begins with an unwavering refusal to give yourself an exit route. You decide that the only outcome you'll tolerate is success. That might sound intimidating, but it's also immensely liberating. You stop leaving the door cracked open for your next failure by releasing that last shred of permission to fail. Some people recoil at the idea because it sounds so final, but that's precisely what gets results. Deny yourself the excuse, and you're already halfway to your goal.

Notice I don't mention blame. Blame is the bleating of the ego, and it's good for exactly nothing. If you needed to run a four-minute mile but broke your leg, that might explain why you failed to meet your goal. But it doesn't change the end result. You still didn't achieve what you set out to do, so ultimately, you can either choose to find a new route forward or wallow in the justification. The question is: do you want to cling to the story of why it's not your fault, or do you actually want results?

Winning is less about brute force than it is about resilience, to paraphrase that famous Rocky quote. If you come up with an excuse—no matter how logical it seems—you're simultaneously admitting you're done trying. You're lying on the mat, waiting for the referee to count you out. Taking a few lumps is part of many transformations. The bigger question is whether you can get up again, rather than how well you dodge every blow.

To be genuinely happy and sober, you need to latch onto the concept that this has to be done for you, for your well-being, for your mental and physical integrity. Not because you feel guilty or because your friends or spouse want you to shape up. The turning point happens when you realize you deserve better than to let a chemical rummage around in your life, messing up your family, your finances, and your peace of mind. If you find yourself lacking that sense of self-love, spend some time reflecting on how you reached this point. But know that it's absolutely key to sustaining real change.

The next practical step can be as simple as grabbing a pen and a sheet of paper. Write down every single reason you currently drink. Don't hold back. If you believe it helps you unwind after a tense day at work, put it down. If you tell yourself you need it to sleep, list that too. Maybe you're convinced it's your only source of joy, your magic elixir for social events, or your remedy for anxiety. Keep going until you run out of excuses or your hand cramps. This exercise may feel silly, but it's crucial. We can't dismantle illusions if they remain swirling vaguely in your mind. Putting them on paper forces you to confront them head-on.

I've heard everything from "It's part of my culture" to "I only do it on weekends, so it's not that bad." Some people talk about how top executives drink, so it must be a sign of success. Others mention how they can't possibly celebrate a wedding or a holiday without a toast of champagne or a spiked eggnog. It's shocking how many rationalizations you can accumulate to protect a toxic habit. But they're all lies, built around a substance that, from a purely scientific standpoint, ranks just below heroin in its addictive potential.

Think about that for a moment. Heroin is widely regarded with fear and revulsion, while alcohol is sold on the same shelf as groceries. We've spent countless generations weaving a tapestry of myths about how harmless or fun it is. Then we wonder why so many people get ensnared. The real power of alcohol lies in how skillfully it conceals its fangs, creeping up on you so slowly that you fail to notice until you're neck-deep in trouble.

It reminds me of that old cartoon image of stepping into quicksand: it's so thick and slow-moving that you don't immediately realize you're sinking. There's no dramatic splash. At first, it feels almost solid underfoot, so you just keep walking. By the time it starts dragging you under, you've ventured too far to scramble back to firm ground. Now, if you thrash and blame everyone else for not warning you, you usually sink faster. The only way out is to calmly figure out how to free yourself—without lies, denial, or anger controlling your actions.

This is the mission I'm inviting you to undertake: recognize that you marched into this trap yourself, knowingly or not, and that you are the person with the power to break free. This might sound harsh at first, but it's also a statement of self-empowerment. If you got yourself into a jam, you can get yourself out. You no longer need to rely on a magic pill or wait for some outside force to rescue you. The solution is inside you: your willingness to do whatever it takes. That might involve reading the rest of this book with an open heart, or joining a program, or seeking therapy that doesn't revolve around labeling yourself an "alcoholic" for the rest of your days.

Now consider the reasons to drink you've compiled. If you said you need it to calm down, examine how well that actually works in the long run. You might achieve a temporary numbness, but the next morning, the stressors are still there, often magnified by a hangover or guilt. If you said you need a drink to fall asleep, recall that boozing before bed actually leads to poor-quality rest, leaving you sluggish and moody the next day. Meanwhile, if you've built your social life around drinking, that might be the hardest illusion to break. Try picturing a social gathering where no one is hammered and see if it's really any less fun. You might be surprised to find that genuine conversations and not dealing with a hangover can be far more rewarding.

Alcohol is stellar at manipulation. It convinces you that it's the missing puzzle piece in your life: the only salve for heartbreak, the only pathway to laughter, the only route to unwind. Yet look at how often it's triggered heartbreak, caused humiliations, or fueled anxiety. If it truly delivered all the wonders it promised, your life should have been a fairy tale by now. Instead, you wind up with fleeting highs, overshadowed by compounding misery. That's the hallmark of every addictive substance: it offers short bursts of relief, followed by deeper holes that demand more of the same substance to fill them.

Society, bizarrely, loves to pretend there's a clean line between "normal" drinkers and alcoholics. But how many normal folks do you know who've had a messy night, said something stupid, or driven when they really shouldn't have because they were under the influence? If we were dealing with a harmless pastime, we wouldn't see so many regrets, accidents, and tragedies. We wouldn't see the police busy with alcohol-fueled fights on a Friday night, nor a spike in domestic violence after big sporting events where drinking is practically mandatory. The lies that big industries pay for—those glossy ads with glamorous couples laughing in swanky bars—are dangerously incomplete. They omit the aftershocks.

Maybe you're now thinking about quitting but you're terrified of missing out. You might picture your future as bleak: no more dinners out, no more fun parties, no more feeling at ease in social situations. But that, too, is an illusion crafted by years of marketing and cultural conditioning. Once you pry yourself away from the cycle, you might realize how much more time, energy, and money you have. You'll wake up each morning without a suffocating hangover, free to do something meaningful. The stiff awkwardness you fear without booze often disappears once you're comfortable in your own skin—a comfort that grows when you stop dulling your senses with a toxin. It can feel jarring at first, but it's astounding how quickly you adapt, especially when you see that life is actually brighter and more vivid without the chemical haze.

You might come across people or groups who claim you must forever refer to yourself as "an alcoholic." That approach fits some folks, especially if they find strength in affirming their condition daily. But I argue that you're not a broken creature who needs to wear that label for eternity. You tried a drug, got hooked, and are now deciding it's no longer acceptable in your life. It doesn't mean you're doomed to white-knuckle your way through each day, craving the stuff. That's the difference between forcing yourself to avoid something you still believe is beneficial versus completely changing how you perceive it.

Imagine a scenario: If you woke up tomorrow and discovered you were allergic to peanuts and they made your throat close up, you probably wouldn't mope for the rest of your life about not being able to enjoy peanut butter. You'd see it as a necessary boundary for your health. With alcohol, the shift can be similar once you fully accept that it's not the pleasurable pastime it pretends to be. It's a hidden threat that can sabotage your well-being and your happiness in a hundred small ways.

The biggest chunk of this transformation is mental. You have to break the illusions built up by your experiences, your social circles, and the media. You dismantle them piece by piece until you realize they're nothing but a stage set. This is what I refer to as discovering that the emperor has no clothes. Alcohol tries to disguise itself as a magical substance, but when you really look at it, all you see is a colorless, foul-tasting poison that humans have dressed up with fruit flavors or elegant labels. The illusions are so strong, though, that you need consistent, methodical dismantling to free yourself from them.

Take a moment to remember how marketing shapes your perception. Ads might show graceful, attractive people swirling brandy in crystal snifters, or comedic parties fueled by beer, but they never show the next morning, with pounding headaches and bank balances that took a hit. They never show the frantic text messages you sent while tipsy, or the argument that erupted over an offhand comment no one would have made if they were sober.

Brands rely on your willingness to forget all that and buy into the fantasy. Yet lies dissolve once you flip the spotlight on them.

If you're still unconvinced and want further proof that alcohol is anything but a cute little social pleasantry, look at the silent devastation it causes across the globe. Broken marriages, abused children, missed workdays, violent outbursts, fatal car accidents, self-loathing, lost ambitions—this litany is endless, and we chalk it all up to individuals who "couldn't handle their drink." But the problem is the substance itself, an addictive agent that hooks us by providing fleeting euphoria at the expense of deeper well-being.

You might be thinking, "What about the worst-case scenario? Even if it gets that bad, I'll just stop." But that's akin to the mouse thinking it can dart away from the trap at the last second, only to discover that once it's sprung, there's no time or space to escape. If you wait until your body is screaming at you, you might already be on a downward spiral. So the safest, most effective strategy is to see the trap for what it is and step away before it slams on you.

Yet the drinking cycle is so ingrained that many people around you might refuse to see it. It's easier for them to maintain the status quo, to reassure themselves they're "normal" because they only binge on weekends or only drink top-shelf whiskey. The beliefs they hold are identical to those that once entranced you—or might still be doing so. The difference is you're now exposing them. That can feel uncomfortable because illusions are comforting, no matter how destructive. But illusions can never serve you for long once you see their cracks.

Consider how you felt the first time you realized a beloved magician's trick was just sleight of hand. There's that initial burst of disappointment, followed by curiosity, maybe even a sense of empowerment that you're no longer fooled.

Alcohol's illusions are similar, but carry much higher stakes. Once you see behind the curtain, you're free to decide that you want no part in the performance.

This is where taking 100% ownership of your life is critical. You got involved with this chemical, you've discovered it's slowly poisoning you, and now you have the option to quit. That's the essence of empowerment. The only "magic bullet" would be a pill that changes your entire psychology overnight, and no, it doesn't exist. The real remedy is your own determination and clarity. You can't purchase it at a store, and you can't rely on your spouse or best friend to do it for you. But once you commit, you'll find that old lies lose their grip surprisingly fast.

People often ask, "Well, what about special occasions? Will I never be able to toast a friend's wedding or sip champagne on New Year's Eve?" Once you fully see alcohol as the adversary it is, you might not even want it. Think about it: do you still have an appetite for raw sewage on a cracker or a teaspoon of bleach for dessert? The comparison might seem extreme, but that's how you'll eventually view these illusions about alcohol. The notion that you need it to celebrate something will feel absurd because you'll no longer see it as a treat—more like a pollutant masquerading as a treat.

It may help to realize that once you remove the toxin, your celebrations become more honest, your connections more genuine, and your body a whole lot healthier. That's not to say you'll never be tempted, especially if friends or cultural habits persist. But every time you step away from the illusions, you reinforce your new perspective, and it becomes easier. One day, the desire simply isn't there, and you're free.

The most critical step is that initial shift, the moment you stop regarding alcohol as some pleasurable commodity that you can't or shouldn't have, and start seeing it as a con artist that's cost you more than you ever gained from it.

From there, you chip away at the illusions day by day. That's how you break free of the loop once and for all. Not by calling yourself an addict forever or chaining yourself to a meeting hall. By recognizing that you have no reason or desire to keep sipping a toxin that's never truly done you any favors.

You may be reading this with skepticism, certain that your situation is special. Maybe you've used alcohol for decades and can't imagine life without it, or you fear you'll crumble under social pressure. Let me assure you, these beliefs are normal. It's easy to treat them as unbreakable truths. But lies are made of the same stuff as nightmares: shadows of thoughts that vanish when confronted with the light. Once you see them as illusions, they no longer have the same power over you.

If you do find yourself longing for a community of people who "get it," they're out there, and many don't demand that you label yourself for the rest of your life. They simply provide understanding, strategies, a place to vent, and the reassurance that you're not alone in dismantling these delusions. If you prefer to go it alone, you'll still find a wealth of books, online courses, and personal development resources that can equip you with everything you need to stand firm in your decision. The important part is that you no longer lie to yourself about what's really going on. You toss away any illusions about "harmless," "normal," or "just one more can't hurt," and you stand unwavering in your new truth.

From my personal journey, I can say with absolute certainty that the illusions we build around alcohol are far more potent than the actual chemical. Once you tear those lies down, the substance itself loses its romantic glow. It becomes about as appealing as a stagnant puddle of dirty water. You might even find yourself amazed that you ever fell for the marketing spin. But we all do, because it's hammered into us from the day we're old enough to notice billboard ads or hear grown-ups talk about "needing a drink." It's no surprise so many get trapped.

At some point, you realize that not only can you escape, but you can thrive outside that loop. Waking up each morning with a clear head and a stable heart might feel surreal at first. Not having to piece together last night's events, not losing hours or days to hangovers, not draining your bank account on an addictive crutch—these can feel like brand-new gifts. Over time, you'll probably wonder why you ever believed you needed the stuff. The illusions might tug at your sleeve from time to time, especially in certain social settings, but once you truly see them as illusions, they hold no real threat. They can't force you to do anything. The choice remains yours.

Chapter 2: Step Away From The Mousetrap!

Picture a scene of an old-fashioned mousetrap, wooden, a bit creaky, and prepped with the biggest chunk of cheese you've ever seen. The mouse skitters up, sees that succulent snack, and can't resist. We don't exactly need Sherlock Holmes to figure out the ending. Whether it's one second or an hour later, that steel bar is going to snap shut. Alcohol is precisely that kind of setup. A lot of people would rather tiptoe around the trap and go for "just a nibble here and there," but if you're addicted, those small nibbles don't exist in reality. There's nothing partial about it. At some level, you're either in that mousetrap or you're out of it. When we're dealing with a substance that hooks into your brain chemistry so effectively, it's the same as saying you can't be "slightly pregnant." If you're dependent on alcohol, you really can't negotiate with it and keep your freedom at the same time.

In many cases, folks need time to reach the realization that total cessation is the only logical option. Sometimes, they'll read a book like this more than once before it sinks in. The important thing is that you eventually come to a place inside yourself where you decide enough is enough. That moment can't be forced on you by your spouse, your friends, or even your doctor. It has to be your own firm conclusion that you're ready to break the cycle for good. If you haven't felt that pull yet—if you're still hanging onto the idea that you "enjoy it too much" to quit—don't use this as yet another stick to beat yourself with. Many people reading these words are in the same boat, still flirting with the notion that maybe they can wrestle the good bits from alcohol while dodging the negative parts. That's natural. We tend to cling to beliefs of control, right up until we see the simple truth: the pleasant aspects and the dreadful consequences are part of the same package, and you can't keep one side without being saddled with the other.

I spent years reaching for every "bucket" I could find, hoping to bail out the sinking Titanic of my drinking habit. Perhaps I'd limit my intake to weekends only, vow not to drink at home, or force myself to alternate water with wine. None of it changed the underlying fact that I still believed alcohol was delivering a benefit—so I kept looking for ways to preserve that alleged upside without tolerating the misery. It was like spinning in circles, watching the hole in the hull let in more water than my hopeful little bucket could remove.

Some of my strategies got genuinely laughable in hindsight. I tried the medication route, trusting chemical interventions like Disulfiram or Acamprosate to solve the puzzle. Disulfiram was especially interesting because it makes you violently ill if you mix it with alcohol. The theory is that this horror show will scare you away from drinking, but it also assumes you'll diligently swallow the pill every morning. For a person with shaky discipline and a love affair with alcohol, that's a big assumption. I rationalized skipping doses if a big event was coming up. Then I decided I "deserved" the weekend off from the medication because I was apparently being such a good boy for five whole days. Eventually, I started seeing just how cunning my mind could be. I even tested the waters to see if I could drink small amounts without paying too steep a price from the medication. Then, one foolish night, I tried a bigger dose of alcohol—trust me, that fiasco ended with my heart hammering so hard in my chest that I worried it might explode. My face was the color of a boiled lobster, and I thought I was going to exit the planet right there in my own living room. You'd assume that would have permanently changed my perspective, but while the memory was horrifying, it still didn't eradicate my belief that alcohol was worth having around.

I tried Acamprosate, which sucked the pleasure out of drinking by interfering with your brain's dopamine response, but that too required daily compliance, plus a range of side effects that made me feel like I had the worst flu in the universe. In the end, I gave up because it felt like I was living half alive, dogged by constant dizzy spells and insomnia. If you approach the problem as something to be solved with willpower—whether that's willpower to swallow a daily pill or to stick to a complicated schedule of self-denial—sooner or later you discover that the essential premise is flawed. No matter what crutches you rely on, as long as you harbor the belief that alcohol is a stolen slice of heaven, you'll always circle back to "just one more."

I'd like to point out that falling off the wagon isn't some cosmic sign that you're doomed. Sometimes, people read a book like this, go a few weeks without touching a drop, and then slip. It's easy to conclude they're a failure or the program "didn't work." That's usually the mind latching onto a story about the future—pretending that last night's slip means you're stuck for all time. By tomorrow morning, that slip is already in the past, which no longer exists anywhere except your memory. It certainly doesn't dictate what you do next. Sometimes we get fixated on the idea that if we messed up once, we might as well throw in the towel. The only real difference between those who ultimately succeed and those who never do is that the successful folks refuse to let a misstep define them. If you wake up hungover after three glorious weeks of sobriety, that doesn't mean the last three weeks were all for nothing. Shake it off and carry on. Your conscious mind has zero capacity to predict the future anyway. You can't see what's around the corner; you can only choose how you respond to this moment.

The secret to changing your relationship with booze is the same principle that gets results in any significant life transformation: a willingness to stay in the present. Worrying that you'll crave a drink on vacation next month or that you can't imagine a New Year's Eve without champagne is your mind trying to forecast scenarios that don't exist yet. To become sober and happy, you remain right here, noticing the urge if it pops up and choosing not to feed it. One day, that urge to drink dissolves into the background like a faint memory of something you once thought was crucial. Trying to guess how you'll behave at your best friend's birthday party in six months is a game the conscious mind loves to play—it drags you into hypotheticals that can swirl you in circles. Let that go. You're living your life now, not in six months' time.

Getting out of the trap involves catching yourself whenever your mind leaps into future scenarios or replays old embarrassments on a loop. Once you recognize that your mind is pulling you toward illusions, you can detach from the drama of it all. You start to see those anxious or regretful thoughts for what they are—just mental chatter. Let them move on through without fixating on them or letting them shape your next choices. Each time you decline to follow your mind down a gloomy rabbit hole, you reclaim a little more of your genuine power. It won't happen overnight, because if you've been addicted for years, you've also spent years building certain mental habits. But with consistent practice, it becomes second nature to swat away the illusions and return to the present moment. Eventually, the panic and predictions evaporate, replaced by a deeper sense of calm.

One question I hear all the time is, "How long does it take?" The short answer is that I'm not psychic, and neither are you. For some people, reading these chapters is enough to cause a lightbulb moment—they no longer see any reason to keep drinking and just stop immediately. Other individuals need weeks or months to let this perspective sink in. A few re-read the text multiple times before the penny drops. That's perfectly fine. Everyone's journey unfolds differently, but if you soak up the core truth that alcohol doesn't deliver any real positives, you eventually reach a tipping point where you simply lose interest in continuing the habit.

A major reason people seek help at all is they've hit a threshold of pain or embarrassment. Perhaps they made an ugly scene at a wedding, or they're hemorrhaging money they don't have on this destructive pastime. The functional problem drinker, on the other hand, might keep going for years without any glaring meltdown that forces them to look in the mirror. If you can still show up to work on time, pay your bills, and hold it together on the outside, it's tempting to believe everything is "fine." Our culture perpetuates this by portraying alcoholics as homeless, stumbling wrecks who can't string a sentence together. In reality, many folks with serious dependencies still dress well, excel in their careers, and show no outward sign of trouble. A film director who wants to show an alcoholic character usually depicts the extreme version for dramatic effect, not the business executive who slings back gin and tonics at home while nobody's watching.

Just because you aren't a "down-and-out" in the park doesn't mean you're free of consequences. The functional alcoholic can do just as much damage to their body as someone with more obvious struggles. Tolerance is a huge red flag: if you need a lot more alcohol to reach the same buzz, it means your body has adapted to this toxin, indicating you've stepped deeper into the trap. There's an old story about a British soap opera actor who consumed nine double vodkas, then drove his car. He claimed in court that he was such a seasoned drinker he could handle it. The judge was actually swayed by the demonstration of his "incredible tolerance" and gave him a lenient sentence. That's like the clown in the circus who can juggle a dozen torches at once—maybe it looks impressive, but you wouldn't want to stand anywhere near him when something eventually goes horribly wrong. Tolerance is an ominous sign, not a superpower.

We need to redefine what "alcoholic" means. People who rail against that word might snap, "I'm not one of those losers." Yet, many have soared through their adult life downing alarming amounts of wine or liquor, while still holding respectable jobs, raising families, and paying the mortgage. The rest of the world may never suspect how much they put away each night. Alcoholism isn't about whether you're sleeping under a bridge with a brown paper bag. It's about the extent to which alcohol is controlling you, even if you're outwardly wearing a shiny façade.

Addiction is not a sign of a weak will or a defective personality. If that were the case, you'd see addicts failing in every area of life. You'd see them all helplessly addicted to every substance and craving out there, from sugary sweets to gambling, but that's not how it works. Each person's chemical and psychological makeup can leave them vulnerable to specific loops. You might be perfectly indifferent to nicotine but entirely undone by a few beers. Another friend could be addicted to cigarettes but rarely touches alcohol. That doesn't prove a moral failing—it shows how differently each of us is wired.

Calling alcoholism a disease can be useful for generating sympathy, but it also fosters the idea that you're powerless—like you caught some virus through no fault of your own, and there's not much you can do about it. Then come the pity parties, where you drown your sorrows in the very substance that's fueling your problems. Does that lead anywhere good? Usually not. The reality is that while you never stood a chance of taming an addictive poison, it's still your responsibility to address the problem now. Getting stuck in self-blame is equally pointless. It's not about punishing yourself; it's about owning the situation. You've been locked in a complicated and cunning loop, but it's also breakable once you see through the lies.

Some of those illusions revolve around convenience. People say they drink to numb their problems, but ironically, alcohol either amplifies those issues or simply shoves them aside for tomorrow with a new layer of misery on top. If you're worried about credit card bills, swigging whiskey each night certainly won't pad your bank account. On the contrary, the cost of your drinking might be exactly why those bills keep stacking up. Or maybe you're stressed at work, so you use alcohol to blow off steam. You might achieve a brief sense of relaxation while the poison squelches your brain function, but next morning, your stress is waiting for you, multiplied by a hangover. The cycle churns on.

Stopping your drinking can bring some immediate and obvious perks, like saving thousands of dollars a year. That's always a nice bonus, but money alone seldom motivates people to stick with sobriety. There's a deeper reason, which you'll hopefully uncover as you keep reading. But it's important not to treat these pages like an instruction manual where you skip around looking for a quick fix. There's no single "aha!" sentence that will cure you by magic. Instead, it's about chipping away at the illusions and layers of conditioning that have propped up your dependence. Once those illusions crack, you won't feel deprived at the thought of not drinking. The whole concept of "cutting down" becomes absurd because you no longer see the allure. You simply step away from the mousetrap and move forward with your life.

People often cling to the notion that a small amount of alcohol can be beneficial. "Red wine is good for your heart," they say, quoting some snippet from a clickbait headline. If wine were truly the best heart medicine, hospitals would be handing it out in the ER. But they're not, because you can get the same heart-friendly antioxidants from grape juice, fresh fruits, or a healthy diet. If you want to keep that argument alive, it might be worth being honest with yourself: maybe it's not about your heart at all. Maybe you just like a reason to hold onto the substance that has embedded itself into your daily routine.

Plenty of drinkers go through a phase where they try to reduce consumption. Perhaps they vow to only drink on weekends, or only after 7 p.m., or only on special occasions. But that approach is like telling your buddy who plays Russian roulette for fun, "Well, just put fewer bullets in the chamber—maybe only on Saturdays." You're still flirting with a loaded gun. In these pages, we're going to lay bare exactly why alcohol doesn't serve you and how it's all smoke and mirrors orchestrated by marketing, society, and a deeply rooted chemical reaction in your own brain. You might find yourself resisting these arguments at first. You might be so wrapped up in the notion that "I need a drink to relax" that you reflexively dismiss any statement to the contrary. Keep going. Even if you feel that reflex, you'll find your worldview starting to shift bit by bit.

When you get down to the core of it, there's only one reason alcohol becomes a problem: it's addictive. A bit like standing under a waterfall and expecting to stay dry, eventually the simple fact that it's addictive wins out. Some claim they have a disease, others say they have an "addictive personality." But if you took an inherently addictive substance on a regular basis, wouldn't it be predictable that you might get hooked?

If you enjoy juggling knives, it's no surprise if you eventually get a nasty cut. It's not that you have a "knife-addictive personality." You played with something dangerous long enough, and the outcome was basically inevitable. Humans have a knack for complicating that which is simple, weaving guilt and shame into the story. But at the end of the day, this is about chemical dependency. You keep picking up the glass, your body and mind adapt to the presence of alcohol, and now you're stuck in a negative feedback loop that escalates over time.

Genetics can play a role in how quickly or intensely you get hooked. Some new research in epigenetics suggests that traumatic experiences and certain predispositions can be passed down through generations in surprising ways. It's possible you got a head start down this path if your ancestors had their own run-ins with alcohol. Even so, that doesn't absolve you of responsibility. If you find out heart disease runs in your family, does that mean you keep eating junk food all day, every day, and then blame mom and dad when the doctor sees you? Ultimately, you still have choices about how you handle your own health.

The big problem for heavy drinkers is that alcohol gradually rewires your brain chemistry. Specifically, it pushes your reward system to release artificial bursts of feel-good chemicals like dopamine, while simultaneously damaging the receptors that process those chemicals. Over time, you develop tolerance and need more booze just to achieve the same sensation. Meanwhile, your body also becomes accustomed to clearing out the poison at a quicker rate, producing additional chemicals like acetaldehyde (which is itself toxic) in large doses. This does a number on your organs, your mental state, and your sense of well-being. You end up stressed out, tired, or anxious, and guess what your mind proposes as a fix? Another drink. It's like trying to extinguish a fire by dumping more kerosene on it because the initial splash of liquid looks cooling for a moment.

If you owned a high-priced racehorse, you'd never dream of pouring poison into its feed. Yet, we treat our own bodies in ways we'd never treat that million-dollar stallion. The difference is, we're hammered from childhood by cultural messages that drinking is normal, sexy, and fun. We see celebrities endorsing champagne as if it's the fountain of youth, or watch countless ads showing smiling people at parties as though their only goal is to find the perfect microbrew. It might all look harmless from the outside, but when you step back, it's breathtaking how thoroughly we've glamorized a substance that kills more people than all the top illegal drugs combined.

When you have a big tolerance, you can pour a lot of liquor into your system without collapsing. That doesn't mean your body is "fine" with it. The damage can be silent but lethal. If you rely on willpower alone to quit, you're basically forcing yourself to ignore your own chemical cravings. That's like trying to outshout an amplified rock concert by whispering. Willpower gets overpowered by the raw biology of addiction, which is precisely why so many attempts at moderation fall flat. Quitting for good requires you to stop regarding alcohol as your friend in the first place. That shift can't happen through blunt force. It comes from learning the truth, letting it percolate, and eventually seeing that alcohol's alleged joys are illusions. Once you see it as a toxic liar, you won't need a pep talk to turn it down. You simply won't want it.

We're so heavily brainwashed to think that drinking is inseparable from happiness, social events, romance, you name it, that the initial prospect of a life without it feels dismal. Some people react by listing all the reasons they could never do such a thing: "I can't attend a wedding sober," or "I'd be so dull at parties," or "I need a glass of wine just to relax at the end of a long day." They're not being disingenuous. They genuinely believe these statements, because that's the program that's been installed in their head by years of repeated use and cultural reinforcement. The only way to dispel these beliefs is to see them for what they are: illusions. If you still accept them as truths, no wonder you feel anxious about quitting.

That's why knowledge is everything here. You don't have to be a chemist to understand that alcohol is a depressant that creates artificial highs and deeper lows. You don't have to be a psychologist to know that if you rely on a substance to deal with stress, you never actually learn coping skills that don't involve alcohol. You don't have to be a doctor to see that alcohol stands behind an alarming number of hospital admissions and fatalities. The more you see behind the curtain, the less magical the drink appears, and the less willpower it takes to say "No thanks."

I'm not speaking from a pedestal. I spent over 17 years wrestling with this drug, making vows in the morning that I promptly broke in the evening. The difference between you and me might be that I'm on the other side of the trap, looking back at you with full empathy for the battles going on in your head. I understand how your mind can want to quit and cling to the idea of never quitting at the same time. When I was in that limbo, I dreaded the thought of never having another drink more than the actual negative consequences. It felt like giving up a best friend or erasing half my personality. If that resonates, there's no need to feel ashamed. Millions of people have been there.

The reason you believe that life without alcohol would be dull, anxious, or colorless is that you're still convinced the substance holds genuine benefits. If you truly saw it as an engine of destruction with zero payoff, you wouldn't be reading these words. You'd have thrown your bottles in the trash long ago. So all the times you say "I can't possibly go on holiday sober" or "I can't picture enjoying myself at a party without a cocktail," that's your mind's old tape playing. Like how people once insisted the Earth was flat, we collectively keep repeating the same mistaken ideas until they're embedded as fact.

Consider how you've never actually seen oxygen itself—yet you don't doubt it's there in the air. You trust the scientists, your teachers, and the repeated statements of friends and family. That's how beliefs get ingrained, and it's precisely how we ended up with the widely accepted myth that "alcohol is essential to a good time." Everyone around you has probably been saying it for decades, so it must be true, right? Well, no. Countless lies become so entrenched that they seem like universal truths until you shine the right spotlight. Sometimes it's a trauma or an epiphany that does the trick; other times it's just consistent reflection. But once you see the delusions, you can't unsee them.

Perhaps you're so ingrained in your illusions that you insist you truly love the taste of raw alcohol. Next time, try sipping it totally neat, without mixers, and see how you feel. Odds are you'll recoil if you're honest with yourself, because pure alcohol is vile, burning your throat and leaving a bitter aftertaste. We usually smother it with sugar, fruit juices, or other flavors so we can get it down with minimal gagging. But if you're at the point of telling yourself, "I love the taste of neat vodka," that might be a sign your illusions are wearing armor. Don't panic if that's the case—just keep reading. There's a reason illusions can become so strong, but beliefs can be dissolved once you recognize them as such.

You might have come across references to the "mousetrap" in other parts of this text. The analogy stands: once you step onto the trap, you're gambling with your well-being. It's a matter of time before the device snaps shut. Some folks get caught fast, others manage to tiptoe around for years, but nobody is truly safe. The marketing messages that saturate our environment, praising the social magic of alcohol, are the reason we keep seeing that cheese as an irresistible treat. But it's always the same outcome in the end if you stay on the board. So the only surefire way to avoid the snap is to stop letting the cheese tempt you in the first place.

Industry regulations give alcohol an almost supernatural level of protection because it's been around forever. If a new chemical with similar effects appeared today, the outcry would be huge, and it would likely get banned in half the world's countries for being dangerously addictive. But since people have been boozing for thousands of years, we're used to it. We sometimes assume that it must be somewhat safe because it's so widespread. This "safety in numbers" mentality is nonsense, though. If a billion people play Russian roulette, the odds for each individual remain exactly as lethal as if they played alone. The next bullet that discharges from your personal gun has nothing to do with how many other people are pulling their triggers at the same time. The illusions that everyone else is "just fine" often hide the fact that many are not so fine after all.

If you picked up this book hoping to discover a way to moderate your drinking, maybe I seem like a party-pooper for asserting that total abstinence is the only real solution. But I can't stand in good conscience and pretend that a perfect compromise is out there, waiting to be discovered. If I told you it might be possible, I'd be reinforcing the lie that alcohol provides some benefit worth salvaging. That would sabotage the entire point of these pages. It would be like telling a smoker that if they cut down to one cigarette a day, it'll be good for them because nicotine has some minor appetite-suppressing qualities. The net outcome is still negative.

There's a well-worn argument about the alleged heart benefits of red wine—its antioxidants or flavonoids. That's true to the extent you can also get those same health benefits from fresh grapes, pomegranate seeds, or numerous fruits and vegetables. If the only reason you're drinking red wine is for your heart, then the moment you realize those same nutrients come from simpler sources should be enough to dismantle that excuse. If you persist in using that argument, it's probably not your heart that's dictating your choices.

When you see that your drinking habit has escalated from a casual "like-to-have" to a desperate "must-have," that's the best time to step back and reevaluate. It's the same as discovering your friend is playing Russian roulette more often than you realized and urging them to stop. You wouldn't say, "Try loading fewer bullets." You'd say, "What on earth are you doing with that gun?" Once the lies are stripped, no rational person clings to the routine of pointing a revolver at their temple and pulling the trigger for fun.

Over the next pages, or as you reflect on these ideas, you'll probably encounter all sorts of evidence about how wonderful those first sips of alcohol are for lightening your mood or helping you mingle at a party. But dig deeper and you'll notice it's all illusions. A lot of it is the mind anticipating the relief of removing the mild withdrawal pang that builds up between drinks. That's like wearing too-tight shoes just so you can savor the feeling when you take them off. If you never wore the shoes in the first place, you'd always feel more comfortable, without that artificial wave of relief.

It's helpful to remember that you weren't born with these illusions. If you handed a glass of brandy to a toddler, they'd likely spit it out in disgust. It's an acquired taste, which you conditioned yourself to tolerate until it became a mental necessity. That took repeated practice—just like learning a language or mastering an instrument. Now you might say, "I love everything about it," but that's the end product of your repeated exposure and social cues, not some fundamental truth.

One huge step to letting go is understanding that the real reason you reach for a drink is that your brain is missing certain chemicals and is under the influence of a toxic loop. If your emotional life feels chaotic, your mind scans for relief and finds it in the short-term numbness alcohol provides. But that numbness is guaranteed to rebound, leaving you even more unsettled once the effect wears off. If you read some of the scientific research on how alcohol depletes or disrupts vital neurotransmitters, you start to grasp why your "nightcap" might make your next day's stress shoot up through the roof. Alcohol gets you once from behind, once from the front, and then circles back to do it again.

If you had a truly valuable resource in your care, like a champion racehorse or a rare violin, you'd never do anything to risk its value. Yet with our own bodies, we pour in toxins and then try to defend the practice by calling it "social drinking." Thanks to millions of years of evolution, the body is resilient, but that resilience can also fool you into thinking you're immune. Meanwhile, your liver might be crying out, dealing with a daily onslaught of poison, and your neurons are gradually losing the ability to regulate themselves. By the time you realize it's serious, you might already be dealing with frightening health problems.

As you come to terms with these illusions, one question might float to the surface: "If willpower can't stop me from drinking, what can?" The answer is that you need to reach a place where you genuinely lose the desire to consume. When you're no longer salivating over a bottle, you don't have to chain yourself to a radiator to avoid it. You can stroll through a liquor store as casually as a vegan walks by the butcher's counter, with zero temptation. That shift isn't about punishing yourself until you conform; it's about reeducating your mind so it sees the false promise of alcohol as something you don't want anymore.

There's also an aspect here where we have to see how alcohol warps the truth. Even those early experiences that felt so magical—like your first real party in college where you laughed with your friends until sunrise—can be illusions. Perhaps you were having fun because you were young, in good company, and free to let loose. Alcohol just happened to be present. But your mind might latch onto the memory as "that was the best time because we were drinking." Could the party have been equally or even more enjoyable if your energy and social connection were natural, instead of chemically distorted?

I'm not a doctor, nor am I a sanctimonious figure who's never made mistakes. I'm just another person who spent far too many years in the exact same loop and now can see it from the outside. I know all about the morning guilt when you vow never to drink again, only to find yourself pouring a glass by evening. I know how your brain can spin and spin, insisting that life without alcohol sounds dull and lonely. The reason you feel that way is because you keep believing the lies that alcohol is a source of comfort and delight. If it were truly as wonderful as your mind claims, we wouldn't see so many shattered families, ruined careers, and tragic ends in hospital wards. We wouldn't have the heartbreak of so many bright, loving people sinking into despair because they can't break free of the chain that's strangling them daily.

You might be reading this and thinking, "But I can't just go to a party sober! People will label me a wet blanket." That's a lie told by your fear. Yes, there might be some folks who think being hammered is the only definition of fun. But are they worth your time if they can't accept you without a glass in hand? And have you ever watched a drunken party from the vantage point of sobriety? It can be both hilarious and sad. The supposed jokes that everyone is cackling at might be nonsense. The "fun" is often sweaty, repetitive chatter, and it ends in hangovers, regrets, or awkward gaffes. Once you're free of the illusion that alcohol is a party essential, you realize that laughter, dancing, and conversation can be even more vibrant when you're not half-numb. Besides, a hangover-free morning is downright blissful.

Another popular line is "I can't relax without a drink." If that were literally true, then your entire capacity for relaxation would hinge on an external poison—a dreadful thought if you imagine being stuck somewhere without it. In reality, your body has its own built-in relaxation system, involving neurotransmitters like GABA and neurochemicals like melatonin. Alcohol disrupts that system. The calm you feel is more a alcohol effect than genuine, restorative peace. You might pass out, but the quality of your sleep is poor, leaving you more stressed in the long run.

If your illusions about alcohol are so well-fortified that you still think I'm spouting nonsense, that's okay. Keep reading, reflecting, or rereading. Slowly, your mind might start to question whether the rules you've grown up believing are as fixed as you once assumed. Over time, you may notice cracks in the beliefs, like the difference between a real holiday you can fully enjoy and a boozy blur that you can barely remember except for the throbbing headache. Or the difference between a calm, stable sense of self-worth and a fleeting numbness that you pay for with sour regret.

Here's something else: the moment you decide never to drink again doesn't mean you're going to become a hermit, or an outcast, or a joyless drudge. In fact, many sober individuals rediscover energies and passions they had sidelined for years. They pick up old hobbies, travel without the burden of lugging around a hangover, connect more deeply with family, and find new ways to handle stress that actually solve the problem instead of deferring it. In a sense, a life without alcohol can be far more expansive because you stop self-sabotaging. Instead of funneling money into a substance that depletes your health, you might spend it on courses, activities, or experiences that genuinely enrich you. It's like stepping out of a dimly lit room into a bright, sunny day.

When your delusions finally crumble, you don't wake up wishing you could drink but valiantly resisting it. You wake up not wanting it at all. That's the difference between willpower-based abstinence and genuine freedom. If you still see alcohol as a precious gem you've heroically decided to forgo, the door remains open for slip-ups. But if you come to see it as a worthless lump of toxic nonsense you're relieved to be rid of, your mind loses all interest in it. That's how the real transformation happens.

If you're concerned about how your social circles will react to your decision, keep in mind that your true friends and loved ones usually prefer a version of you who's fully present and healthy. If anyone pushes you to drink, it might be because they feel uneasy about their own relationship with alcohol. Misery loves company, especially among those clinging to illusions. But your life is yours, and you owe it to yourself to break free from a trap that saps your vitality and peace.

You could read these words a hundred times, but the moment they click with your inner wisdom changes everything. Sometimes that moment arrives as a gentle epiphany in the quiet hours; other times it's a bolt of realization after an especially disastrous night. Regardless of how or when it occurs, the game is up once you see the whole picture. You can't unlearn the truth about the lies. It might take a little while to unravel all the knots, but the direction forward is clear.

None of this is about shaming or calling you weak for falling into a well-laid trap that snared millions before you. It's about extending a hand to say there's another way. There's a way that doesn't involve white-knuckling your urges, a way that doesn't rely on complicated pills that make you violently ill or dull your brain. That way begins with unraveling every story you've ever told yourself about the joys of drinking, gently but firmly showing you how those stories are built on a house of cards. Once you see that house of cards for what it is, it collapses with minimal effort on your part.

It's also not about being some sort of superior being who never touches a substance. It's simply about respecting that we're dealing with a powerful, addictive chemical. If you were allergic to peanuts, you wouldn't mope every time someone else enjoyed a handful. You'd shrug and accept that you can't partake. You'd probably be grateful that you know enough to keep yourself safe. Alcohol is more than just an allergen, of course—it's a universal poison with a cunning streak. But the principle is the same. No sense wishing your body would handle the poison better. It's far more liberating to appreciate that you're better off without it altogether.

Don't let the illusions of your past overshadow the potential brightness of a sober future. If you try socializing a few times without a drink, you might be astonished by how quickly you adapt. If you spend one vacation fully sober, you might realize it's more engaging than you'd imagined possible, with full days of exploring instead of sleeping off a hangover. If a stressful day at work hits and you don't pop open a beer the moment you get home, you might notice that the tension fades naturally in time, leaving you more resilient for the next challenge.

Alcohol tries to hijack your mind by claiming it's your best friend, your only route to celebration, your sole comfort in stress. But a friend doesn't steal from you behind your back, wreck your health, and isolate you from your own children. A friend doesn't demand your money, dignity, and longevity just to spend a little more time together. Alcohol is more like a sneaky con artist who sweet-talks you while emptying your wallet, sabotaging your job, damaging your body, and eroding your sense of self. The moment you spot the con, it can't keep tricking you.

If you start to see through the illusions, keep going. Don't worry about missteps or how many times you have to re-learn the same lesson. Every slip is just a piece of data. Maybe you pick up a glass again, only to rediscover how awful it feels the next morning. That's another confirmation that the illusions are illusions. Eventually, the confirmations stack so high that continuing to drink becomes unthinkable. You won't mourn it; you'll say good riddance. That's not a matter of willpower. It's a matter of clarity.

By reading this far, you're already doing something many never do. You're exploring the possibility that everything you thought you knew about alcohol might be built on false premises. That makes you braver and more open-minded than you might give yourself credit for. And if you keep exploring, keep questioning, and keep challenging the lies, you'll find yourself stepping out of the mousetrap, leaving the cheese behind. One day you'll look back and wonder how you ever believed it was worth tiptoeing around that contraption in the first place. You'll see it for the cheap con it always was.

Chapter 3: The Illusion Of The Evil Clown?

It's fascinating to watch the people who truly break free from alcohol and live authentically sober. They often treat their sobriety the way some individuals embrace a vegan lifestyle or a devout spiritual path. That doesn't mean they never get the fleeting thought, "Maybe a single glass of wine would be nice," any more than a hardcore vegan never has a momentary whiff of bacon that makes their stomach rumble. The difference is that the fleeting urge remains just that—an idle thought that doesn't materialize into a genuine compulsion. They're so secure in their perspective on alcohol that it becomes woven into their identity, as ingrained in their moral code as loyalty to a friend or fidelity to a partner.

Sometimes I meet people who keep trying to use brute force willpower to subdue their drinking habit. They post in forums or mention in conversation, "I made it through Saturday night without cracking open a bottle!" or "I was doing well, but I caved and had a few beers last night." Then come the encouraging responses from others, "Hey, don't be too hard on yourself. At least you lasted a week without drinking." Although these comments are meant to soothe guilt, I can't help but notice the fundamental misunderstanding lurking beneath them. If you find yourself congratulating someone for surviving a short period without alcohol, you're missing the bigger picture of how this addictive substance really operates. Alcohol doesn't mind you avoiding it for a handful of days. That might even strengthen its grip, because each time you go cold turkey for a bit, you may eventually come back at it with a vengeance.

When teetotalism is integrated into your life philosophy, there's no sense of "waiting for the weekend to end so I don't have to battle temptation." You stop viewing booze as a forbidden fruit you secretly crave. It's more like how a vegan rarely says, "Thank goodness I survived another two days without scarfing down a steak." Not eating meat is simply part of who they are. Yes, I'm fully aware that alcohol can hook you chemically, whereas bacon can't rewire your neurotransmitters to the same extent. The point is that once you reframe alcohol in your mind so it's as off-putting to you as a leather jacket is to an ethical vegan, you remove the exhausting element of willpower from the equation.

It's crucial to accept that years (or decades) of drinking will have reshaped your brain. There is no returning to moderate social drinking once you have crossed that invisible line where alcohol lights up your neurons like fireworks on New Year's Eve. Some folks claim that neural pathways can revert to their pre-alcoholic state. In practice, while the body can heal in remarkable ways, any subsequent exposure to alcohol can trigger old patterns instantly. Knowing this, you face a choice: you can trudge along in misery, feeling you're forever deprived of the one thing you love most, or you can adjust your perspective until this sedative drug becomes as revolting to you as the notion of wearing fur might be to someone who values animal welfare.

On the journey away from alcohol, stay alert to the endless lies your own addicted mind will whisper. It can conjure up some wonderfully inventive reasons to keep you pouring that next drink. Most revolve around fear, or as the old acronym states: F.E.A.R = False Evidence Appearing Real. One common example is the belief that you're cursed with an "addictive personality," so perhaps all of this is simply beyond your control. When you decide that your parents, your environment, or some unsympathetic medical community is to blame, you're giving alcohol a perfect smokescreen. It's not about apportioning blame, anyway. No one is personally at fault here—not your mother, not your father, not even you. Yet at the same time, you remain the one who must solve it. Nobody can parachute into your life and permanently fix this for you. You can access resources, advice, or step-by-step guidance, but ultimately, it's your daily commitment that conquers this problem.

I often hear people defend their belief in an addictive personality by pointing out they can't seem to control themselves around chocolate, gambling, or any number of vices. Truth is, you can stroll into a rehab center and find a wildly diverse mix of ages, races, professions, and personality types. Alcohol is an equal-opportunity trap, hooking anyone who's regularly ingesting this chemical. If "addictive personality" truly existed in the way people think, we'd see the same person hopelessly addicted to sweets, cigarettes, meth, and bubble gum all at once. Alcohol, however, preys on a chemical vulnerability in the human brain—something that affects nearly every demographic. That's why you might see a high-powered CEO passing out on a million-dollar yacht, or a homeless individual huddled under a blanket with a paper bag, both undone by the same substance.

The moment you attribute your drinking to an external factor or say, "It's my faulty genetics," you hand yourself permission to fail. That's a dangerous path to walk. It's much more effective to acknowledge that, while you didn't intend to end up in this predicament, you're the only one with the power to climb out. Trying to pin your hope on the idea of an addictive personality is a neat scapegoat, but it doesn't serve your ultimate aim of escaping alcohol's hold.

I recall a peculiar sight in the mid-1980s when a friend's father brought a new computer to his business. They literally had to lift the entire roof off the building to accommodate this gigantic contraption, and a crane hoisted it inside. The machine consumed an entire office and performed no more tasks than a modest calculator. Meanwhile, these days, we toss around mobile phones containing more computing horsepower than the original NASA missions. It's mind-blowing to compare the grand predictions from decades ago—like how some experts once declared there might be a world market for only five computers total. The notion of making a device that weighed "just under one-and-a-half tons" was heralded as a futuristic marvel.

Yet with all that technical progress, we've barely tapped into the capabilities of the human brain—arguably the most advanced processor in existence. We can spend a few years studying complex programming languages and end up writing software that can do extraordinary things, but we can spend an entire lifetime barely scratching the surface of our own mind. A principle in computing known as GIGO, which stands for Garbage In, Garbage Out, reminds programmers that input quality determines the output. The same logic applies to your subconscious. If your mind has received a steady stream of flawed beliefs and beliefs about alcohol, the outcome is quite predictable: destructive loops, addictive behaviors, and rationalizations that keep you stuck.

If you're overweight, your mind might carry a hidden belief that you want (or deserve) to remain that way. If you're attached to alcohol, your subconscious has come to believe that booze is the best or only way to address certain emotional pains or daily stresses. But let's remember that you can't possibly know everything stored in your subconscious any more than you could bottle the entire ocean in a small jar. So it might sound ridiculous to say, "Your subconscious actually wants you to be overweight," or "Your subconscious wants you to binge drink." But at a fundamental level, the code in your mental programming might be reinforcing the exact behaviors you consciously claim to despise.

Dependency on alcohol or other substances often arises from an unconscious calculation that these chemicals ease the discomfort generated by your conscious thoughts. The egoic mind might whisper, "I'm miserable, and a bottle is the quickest fix." Then it repeats that message enough times that it becomes a blueprint for how you cope with stress, heartbreak, or anxiety. The tragedies multiply when your ego latches onto illusions of status, believing that an expensive sports car or a flashy watch or a well-stacked liquor cabinet equates to significance. If left unchallenged, these lies run amok.

The ego fixates on anything that seems to grant a sense of security or dominance. It's like a cowardly guard dog that barks at every rustle, thinking it's the grand protector of your life, but in reality, it's motivated by raw fear. Once the ego's desires become engraved in your subconscious, that's when things become truly damaging—because the subconscious mind is incredibly powerful, while the ego is more like a hyperactive child with a plastic sword. The mismatch in power is huge, and yet the child demands to be in charge.

Sometimes I hear the question: "If the subconscious really holds all this power, why on Earth would it allow us to indulge in destructive habits, like problem drinking?" The best analogy might be that the subconscious is a silent, loyal machine designed to execute whatever programs it's been given. It doesn't judge those instructions—it merely carries them out. If you feed it negative coding, like telling yourself "I'm worthless without a drink in my hand," that message eventually seeps into the subconscious, which then does its best to keep you aligned with that script.

Conventional wisdom states the human mind is divided into the conscious (the smaller piece) and the subconscious (the vast remainder). A tiny fraction of your mental processes is taken up by the chatter of your conscious mind—like a noisy, yapping dog that insists it's in control.

When you were a child, if you stood at the starting line of a race, the ego might have whispered, "You're the fastest kid here—go for it," or "You've got zero chance," shaping your performance regardless of your real abilities. The more you listen to that voice and let it define your experiences, the more entangled it becomes with your sense of self. Before long, many of us can't separate the ego's monologue from our deepest identity. That's where the trouble really starts, because the ego is constantly evaluating, criticizing, and craving. It's rarely content.

Books like The Secret encourage positive thinking to override negative patterns, but that often boils down to willpower arguments against the ego. You might stand in front of the mirror and chant, "I am successful, I am wealthy," but if your subconscious is loaded with the code "I will never amount to much," your positive affirmations might not stick. The real key is aligning the subconscious with your conscious desires. If your subconscious mind believes that you can exist as a content, thriving non-drinker, then your daily reality will begin to reflect that truth effortlessly.

An important saving grace: the subconscious is also responsible for all the wonders your body accomplishes around the clock. You don't consciously command your heart to keep beating, nor your skin to regenerate. The subconscious handles billions of tasks with staggering accuracy, while the ego stands around, wagging a finger, thinking it's in charge. If you tried to consciously manage your digestion, you'd be in trouble before finishing this sentence.

So why do most people turn to alcohol as their "solution"? Because the conscious mind, which is intrinsically neurotic, generates enormous frustration and then tries to silence the discomfort. A shot of whiskey or a glass of wine can briefly numb that maddening voice. You get a fleeting calm, but it's an illusion, because as soon as the buzz fades, the anxiety or dissatisfaction is still there—plus any new problems the drinking brought along, like guilt, fuzzy recollection, or physical hangovers.

If you observe monks or seasoned meditators, they tend not to wrestle with these addictions in quite the same way, precisely because they don't identify so strongly with the ego's demands. They practice staying rooted in the present moment, acknowledging that the past is gone and the future doesn't exist yet. The ego hates that, because it thrives on fear and regrets. People who live mostly in the now find it easier to notice negative impulses as passing clouds rather than all-consuming truths.

For most of us, though, the ego's hold is strong. We carry regrets about the past and anxieties about tomorrow, swirling in a relentless storm. The conscious mind tries to organize this chaos, to line up each potential catastrophe and handle it, but it's impossible. Overwhelmed by a thousand "what ifs," we reach for something—anything—to dull the tension. That's how you end up stepping into the quicksand of addiction, day by day, rationalizing each new glass. You get a few hours' reprieve. Then the same problems remain, joined by the additional headache of dependence.

Now you might see why telling yourself, "I'm just going to use willpower to quit," hardly ever works. If you walk around believing alcohol is your best friend, or that it's essential for coping with tough days, or that it's your only route to social confidence, you're still handing the ego the same script. Trying to forcibly suppress the drinking while your subconscious still endorses it is akin to chaining yourself to a radiator to keep from raiding the liquor cabinet. It can be done for a while, but it's exhausting, and the moment you slip, the ego roars back with renewed strength.

We also carry this moral baggage—if you're struggling with drinking, you might assume it means you're a bad person or a weak one. But it's simply the predictable outcome of ingesting an addictive substance. Nobody beats themselves up when a sleeping pill makes them drowsy, so why do we flog ourselves when a recognized sedative like alcohol sinks its claws in? That said, it's still your job to correct course, because the alternative is to let yourself remain trapped, which rarely leads anywhere you want to go.

In many ways, your drinking pattern is just a symptom of a deeper imbalance—namely, your mind is at war with itself, caught in illusions and restlessness. If you peel back enough layers, you'll notice the true culprit is the ego and its perpetual need to manage everything. Alcohol is just the band-aid it latched onto. Yes, genetic factors might make you more susceptible, or environment might push you toward heavy drinking. But the ultimate root is the ego's mania, which you're trying to soothe or distract.

Everything from worry to depression to anger arises when your conscious mind pretends it can see the future or rewrite the past. It's absurd when you think about it: the only genuine slice of time you ever occupy is right now. People who manage to exist fully in the present moment often have far fewer compulsions, because they're not lost in a swirl of regrets or fears. The rest of us keep believing the ego's illusions, missing the fact that life is happening here and now, not in some imaginary tomorrow.

Yes, it might sound a bit strange or even contradictory, but the ego's big flaw is that it wants to line up your entire future like dominos so that nothing bad could possibly happen. The minute it senses a lack of control, it panics. That panic feeds the impulse to soothe yourself, which often leads to addictive behavior. It's a vicious cycle. You might not see yourself as a prime candidate for Buddhist wisdom or spiritual retreats, yet the core principle is relevant: when the chatter in your mind calms down, your addiction to alcohol becomes far less enticing. You don't need alcohol if you're not drowning in incessant mental noise.

We can also address the physical aspect: your brain chemistry literally shifts under consistent alcohol use. Some people, due to genetics or repeated exposure, produce a massive surge of dopamine at the first sip, while others hardly notice a thing. For you, that rush might have been like the best party trick on Earth—a wave of warmth and euphoria, enough to overshadow the cost. And so you kept going, eventually damaging the receptors that respond to dopamine. Now you need even more liquor to chase the same initial glow. If someone else gets a small dopamine bump from half a glass of wine, they can easily stop. But if you require triple the volume to reach a similar state, the risk of addiction skyrockets.

It's tempting to say, "Well, that's not my fault. I'm just wired this way." True, you might be wired to get a bigger dopamine surge from drinking, but that doesn't mean you can't choose to step away entirely. It's the difference between acknowledging you have a predisposition and letting it define you. If heart disease runs in your family, that might be a reason to take better care of your diet, not an excuse to eat fried food every day. The genetic factor simply explains why you're more likely to get hooked on alcohol. It doesn't condemn you to remain hooked forever.

Even if the original intense buzz from your first months of heavy drinking has faded, the memory of it may linger in your subconscious, painting alcohol as an oasis in a desert of stress. So each time you feel anxious or restless, your mind conjures up, "Hey, remember how that glass used to make everything better?" This is precisely why purely logical arguments or scolding from friends rarely change a drinker's behavior. Deep down, your subconscious believes alcohol is a magical fix. Until that script changes, you're going to keep repeating the cycle.

A simpler reframe is to realize that this entire fiasco is the fault of the drug, not some moral failing in you. Drinking a substance designed to block certain neurotransmitters and flood you with others is bound to create dependence if used frequently enough, especially if your environment or genetics make the door wide open. That alone doesn't make you a wretched human being. But it does make you responsible for pivoting into a better path. Alcohol might have seduced you with illusions, but illusions can be dismantled.

I've watched countless people, including those in high-stress jobs or with families to support, do exactly that. Initially, they're afraid. They imagine life without booze as bleak, a place of forced abstinence and no fun. Over time, though, they see how much more fulfilling each day can be when they're not wrestling with hangovers or guilt or memory gaps. They learn how to handle stress in healthier ways, from exercise to mindfulness to creative outlets. If the ego's voice had been screeching about how impossible life is, they learn to witness that voice from a distance and realize it's just a chatterbox with no real authority.

One vital piece is to lose the lies, not just about alcohol, but about yourself. If you define yourself as a damaged soul who can't cope without a daily drink, you feed that narrative. If you refuse that story, if you say, "I am not an 'alcoholic,' I'm a person who got stuck in a loop," you might find a new sense of strength. You're not lying to yourself or minimizing the problem. You're simply refusing the identity label that perpetuates the belief you're broken. Instead, you focus on the present moment: right now, you're reading, you're breathing, you're alive, and you don't actually need a drink in this second. That's where everything starts—today, this hour, this breath.

Having walked this path myself, I realize how weird it might feel to step outside the loop of boozing. You might think, "But all my friends drink," or "I'll never have fun at parties." Those are delusions too. You might notice many "friends" fade away when you stop partaking in the group's favorite pastime, but your real relationships get stronger. Parties without alcohol can still involve laughter, dancing, or conversation—just without the embarrassing slurs or next-day regrets. The neural torment you put yourself through imagining a life of dryness melts away when you actually experience the upsides of sobriety. Suddenly, you're saving money, you're more present with your children, your body feels more energetic, and your mind is sharper. Once those benefits register deep enough, your subconscious realizes you're not losing anything by skipping the bottle—you're gaining an unburdened life.

The moral dimension of this is simply that you owe yourself an honest assessment. If, after deep reflection, you still think the short-term buzz justifies the long-term heartbreak, that's your call. But if you sense that you were always worthy of a brighter, freer existence, maybe you can let the beliefs die, one by one. No new illusions are required. You don't need to spin stories about how you loathe the taste or how you're far superior to drinkers. You need to see that your old illusions—those about how essential alcohol is—were never based in reality. Once you're done feeding that particular script, alcohol's hold on you becomes unsteady, then it collapses.

I suggest you watch out for moments when the mind tries to build illusions again. Sometimes you might get a subtle cue, like the smell of a certain drink or the memory of a fun evening when you drank without consequence. The ego might pop up to say, "Just one, for old times' sake." If you're practiced at noticing lies, you'll see that voice as an intruder, not a friend. The passing urge might stir something in you, but it won't sink its roots in. You might even smile, recognize the trick, and continue about your business. Life goes on. The moment passes, and you remain free.

It helps to remember that the fundamental nature of illusions is fragility. They need constant reinforcement. The liquor industry invests fortunes in ads and marketing to replenish these illusions. Scenes of glamorous dinner parties, successful executives pouring cocktails, or smiling couples sharing a champagne toast on a yacht. But that's the highlight reel. Missing from the glossy montage is the next morning's headache, the fight that erupted at 2 a.m., the hospital bills from a drunk-driving accident. The beliefs rely on you not seeing the full picture. Once you do, there's no going back to naive enchantment. You might remember the old illusions, but you won't be fooled by them anymore.

All these reasons explain why willpower-based approaches—like just forcing yourself not to drink—feel miserable. If you still believe you need or want alcohol, then not drinking it is a self-imposed punishment. Every day you resist is a day of tension, and eventually that tension typically breaks. But if you shift your perspective so that you see zero genuine advantages in the bottle, quitting becomes a natural byproduct. You can't be deprived of something you no longer desire. This is the real aim, and it's not rocket science—once lies are stripped away, your subconscious rewrites the program. If you're not constantly feeding your mind with that old story about the joys of drinking, your mind no longer craves it like a crucial resource.

If you prefer to do it gradually, or re-read these pages to let the ideas sink in, that's fine. Some people experience an overnight revelation, while others chip away at illusions over weeks or months. The important part is that you keep going until you've dismantled them all. You might find that your addiction tries last-ditch maneuvers—maybe it encourages you to blame your parents or claim you were born to fail. Take a breath, see that for the nonsense it is, and move on.

It can help to see the entire process as peeling away layers of falsehood. This is about returning to the real you—someone who's inherently capable of living life without alcohol. When your mind is quiet, your body is healthy, and your relationships are sincere, you may wonder what you ever saw in that liquid. The prospect of being tipsy might strike you as a weird relic of an older version of yourself, like rummaging through an attic and finding a dusty relic that no longer has any use. You appreciate it for what it taught you about illusions, then you let it go.

When people talk about a chemical imbalance, they usually refer to how alcohol fiddles with neurotransmitters in your brain, forcing a dopamine spike or alcohol effect. That imbalance is real, but it's also correctable. The deeper imbalance might be the mental swirl you get lost in, the illusions you chase, the stories you spin about how you can't handle stress without a drink. If you rectify that, you solve the real puzzle. Then the body's chemistry can recalibrate, giving you a shot at feeling genuinely good—without doping yourself with ethanol.

You might be at a point in life where you've tried everything—pills, expensive rehabs, vows sworn in tears.

Yet the same cycle keeps repeating. There's no shame in that. You approached the problem from a vantage that left the illusions intact. Once you target those delusions directly, you'll find that the grip of alcohol was never as absolute as it seemed. The key is to see, at a very deep level, that you no longer believe a single thing the lies proclaim.

At one point, you probably saw your father or your friends or glamorous TV stars drinking and concluded that it must be a normal, beneficial thing to do. Now you're discovering it was all a grand con. That's okay. That's progress. People once thought the earth was flat or that bigger computers were always better. We learn, we adapt. Shattering beliefs doesn't make you less of a person; it might be one of the bravest transitions you'll ever make.

Keep an eye out for your own self-talk in the days ahead. If you catch your inner voice trying to romanticize "just one glass," step aside mentally and examine the thought. Where's it coming from? Does it hold any water, or is it just more fear-based nonsense? As soon as you realize it's nonsense, the craving evaporates. It might take repeated recognition, but each time you do it, you strengthen the subconscious program that says, "Actually, I'm doing great without that poison."

In the end, you owe it to yourself to see that alcohol isn't some unstoppable force. It's a widely available sedative with a lot of hype. Like any sedative, it can numb you for a while, but it never solves anything. If it did, you'd be living in paradise by now. Ask yourself: are you? Or has it been a repetitive cycle of short-term relief followed by deeper regrets?

When the illusions finally crumble for good, you'll never want to go back. There's a relief in living life with clarity. You might still recall a time when booze felt like a best friend, but that memory will lack any real emotional pull. You'll sense how it was all an elaborate charade, propped up by cultural myths and your own subconscious confusion. That's the moment you walk away from the clownish carnival for good, step into the daylight, and carry on with your life—healthier, wiser, and infinitely more at peace.

Want to make this easy? Find out more about the world's most successful and respected quit drinking course here: https://www.stopdrinkingexpert.com/

Chapter 4: The Stupid Genius

If you have been drinking heavily for several years, it doesn't matter how much success you have achieved. It's still at least 30% less than you were capable of. Alcohol makes you a more stupid version of your best self. I have demonstrated that to be true myself on numerous occasions. I remember one time I was flying from London to New York.

If anyone had spotted me on that flight, they might have wondered why I wore such a massive grin. I'd found my seat in business class and leaned back as though I was the happiest man on Earth. In my head, I pictured myself glowing with confidence and sophistication, but the reality may have been different—probably slurred speech and a glassy stare if you asked the cabin crew. I can't confirm which was more accurate, but I can explain why I was so strangely pleased with myself.

This was in the days when I still drank heavily. The reason I'd splashed out on the pricey upgrade from economy had almost nothing to do with comfort and everything to do with the free-flowing booze. I'd rationalized it as a special treat, as though I deserved that extra luxury. But deep down, I was mostly just chasing the limitless supply of top-shelf liquor from the airport lounge through to landing at JFK. Before I even stepped onto the plane, I was in the British Airways lounge ignoring the pastries, coffee, and the concept of time—it was 9:30 in the morning, but I was at the bar. I pretended not to see my watch, convinced myself that a tumbler half-full of whiskey was a perfectly acceptable breakfast beverage. It wasn't. But illusions have a way of bending logic so convincingly that we start believing the absurd.

Let's consider how alcohol can hijack our reasoning like that. Ever read about how it disrupts normal brain function and effectively saps away your ability to think critically? From a neurochemical standpoint, drinking impairs the prefrontal cortex, the part responsible for rational decision-making, impulse control, and forward planning. Alcohol also tampers with neurotransmitters that regulate mood, so you end up feeling euphoric or unstoppable—at least until the buzz fades. It's not that you're genuinely more creative or confident; it's that your normal filters and cautionary processes switch off, so your illusions run the show. That's the essence of how booze can trick you into ignoring red flags, logical constraints, and even the basic reality that you're ingesting a toxin. This mental glitch might feel wonderful in the moment, but it's basically your intelligence being subdued.

I carried that subdued intelligence straight down the jet bridge and onto my flight, feeling like some sort of triumphant king. The flight attendant smiled politely, handed me a flute of champagne as I settled in, and I recall thinking, "Yes, life is amazing, look at me." The seat belt signs flicked on, the engines roared, and I soared into the sky enveloped in an alcoholic haze of pride and euphoria. My mind soared even higher than the aircraft, buzzing with illusions: that I was a big success, that I could solve any problem. I like to call that little mental trick "sedated grandiosity," the phenomenon where you believe everything's going brilliantly because your mind is half-asleep yet handing you dreams as though they're reality.

It's not unlike what scientists note about how alcohol lowers your inhibitions and turns off your self-critical voice. Usually, that self-critical voice is what helps you spot nonsense or keeps you in check. Under alcohol, the voice is gone. Hence your intelligence—especially your introspective, rational intelligence—slips away. My rational brain was absent that day at 35,000 feet, which is how I ended up constructing what I thought was the greatest business plan of all time. The plan, in my mind, would turn me into a billionaire (not just a millionaire—my lies soared that high). If I'd had Wi-Fi, I might have emailed powerful acquaintances and roped them into my ridiculous scheme. Thank goodness the plane had no internet. The next day, sobered up in a hotel room, I reread my so-called brilliant plan. It was utter gibberish. Not a single sentence made sense. It's amazing how illusions can do that. Alcohol had stolen my capacity to assess the words on the screen with any hint of logic.

That theft of intelligence extends beyond such comedic episodes. If you're using alcohol daily, your baseline clarity is compromised. Brain imaging studies show that chronic alcohol consumption shrinks certain regions of the brain—particularly those linked to memory and higher reasoning. Plus, it disrupts neurogenesis, the creation of new brain cells. People sometimes joke about booze "killing brain cells," but there's a disturbing nugget of truth behind that quip: alcohol over long periods lessens your cognitive resilience. The illusions you carry about alcohol's "benefits" are fueled by the very mental faculties that alcohol impairs. You think you're quite clever ordering a double scotch at 9:30 a.m., but in reality, your normal risk assessment skills have gone on holiday, leaving you convinced it's the best of all possible ideas. That's how the evil clown quietly sabotages your problem-solving and keeps the drug in your life.

After the in-flight meal, I recall finishing the dessert wine, nodding in satisfaction, and thinking, "I'm unstoppable." The evil clown continued to sweet talk me. My notion of success, of creativity, reached an absurd apex. Let's call it alcohol-induced arrogance. I typed furiously for two hours, convinced I was producing Shakespearean-level brilliance. The flight attendant would periodically top up my glass, or offer me something stronger. I kept saying yes. With each drink, the beliefs gathered steam. Of course, physically, my body was busy fighting the toxins, but the illusions told me all was well. Then I dozed off, still imagining how I'd revolutionize my industry. The next morning, faced with that business plan's fiasco, I felt humiliation. The delusions had melted away, replaced by a more potent reality check.

In a sense, lies about alcohol are akin to a dream you know is false, but you can't stop indulging because the dream feels so pleasurable or comforting. It's the same reason we might, in a half-awake state, enjoy a moment of imagining ourselves winning the lottery or being best friends with a movie star. When reality sets in, there's that twinge of disappointment. But illusions about alcohol carry a steeper cost than fleeting disappointment: they can lead you to blow money, sabotage relationships, text ex-partners with cringe-worthy messages, or lose large chunks of your life to an inebriated blur. That's a price that starts to feel exorbitant once you realize what you're giving up.

Many of us have done that classic drunk text to an ex we swore never to speak to again. We conveniently forget how awful the breakup was, how irredeemably toxic the relationship became. Alcohol hushes your rational memory and magnifies the small fraction of nostalgia that pictures candlelit dinners or inside jokes. It's not that you want them back; it's that alcohol robs you of the ability to weigh the reasons you parted in the first place. You wake up the next morning, check your phone in horror, and realize illusions have once again cost you pride or a moment of peace.

This phenomenon of alcohol ripping away your intelligence extends to more subtle areas, too. I've worked with plenty of bright, accomplished individuals—doctors, entrepreneurs, lawyers—who remain baffled at their own daily alcohol. They're good at strategizing, problem-solving, and excelling in their careers, yet they keep falling for garbage about how drinking helps them relax or keep up in social circles. One might imagine well-educated people would see through the lies, but alcohol plays no favorites. Even if you're brilliant in your field, alcohol hijacks your mental circuits once you put enough of that chemical in your body. That's why you see surgeons or judges who quietly battle heavy drinking behind the scenes. It's not for lack of knowledge; it's for lack of clarity once alcohol takes hold.

Now, you might ask: "Why do our incorrect programs around this drug hold such power?" Part of it is that alcohol manipulates the reward pathways in the brain, artificially boosting dopamine levels at the start. For a while, you feel good—like you discovered a quick trick to banish worry or summon confidence. But the body fights back with a wave of aftereffects: mild withdrawal, grogginess, stress. Yet illusions frame those aftereffects as life being tough, so you need to drink again. You start chasing that initial positive sensation, ignoring that it's ephemeral. It's quite the cunning trap: alcohol robs you of intelligence, which in turn makes you more susceptible to illusions, which then keep you using alcohol. A perfect feedback loop.

Let's talk about the real tragedy behind listening to the evil clown: the lost time. Maybe you're not writing worthless business plans at 35,000 feet every day. But how many nights do you zone out on the couch, glass in hand, telling yourself it's the best way to unwind? Hours pass, the alcohol thickens, and you doze off, missing out on a meaningful conversation with a partner or a moment to read a bedtime story to your child. Perhaps you don't remember half of what you watched on TV. Maybe you were too drunk to realize your teenager was hinting they needed to talk about something. Time slips away into an inconsequential haze. Years can disappear like that, overshadowed by delusions that alcohol offers relief. Then one day you realize you can't quite recall the last time you went to bed feeling genuinely peaceful without that crutch.

It's akin to dreaming in bed for an entire day, enthralled by a sweet fantasy. But eventually, you do wake up. And you find that the day is gone—family members, events, personal growth all marched on while you snoozed. That's the real cost of alcohol. The moment you awaken is seldom comfortable, because it reveals how much you let slip away under alcohol's watch. Yet, confronting that awakening can open your eyes to what's still possible.

I used to lament, "Look at all the years I wasted!" The clown tried to spin that regret as a reason to keep drinking: "You've missed so much, so might as well keep going." Another con. If the evil clown loves one dimension, it's negativity. It feeds off your sense that all is lost, so alcohol might at least numb the pain. The more negativity you feel, the more you retreat into alcohol. Another cycle. Breaking free means understanding that alcohol wants you to believe the lie that intoxication is your ally. In truth, addiction is the sly trickster urging you to keep doping yourself to handle the self-inflicted misery alcohol helped create.

So how do we break beliefs' hold on intelligence? It starts by seeing them for what they are. Notice each time you romanticize alcohol. Watch how your mind leaps to the notion, "I deserve a little treat after a rough day." Realize that the treat is just alcohol, not a genuine reward. Call out illusions like you'd call out a magician's sleight of hand. Once you see how the trick is done, it loses power. The lies can't stand scrutiny. They thrive in that half-dazed acceptance you have when alcohol dulls your critical thinking. By shining a spotlight on them while sober, you begin to unravel them.

That might mean writing down the lies of the clown as they appear: "I believe I need alcohol to socialize." Then calmly dissect them. Is that truly so? Don't you handle interactions at work perfectly fine without alcohol? Or maybe you fear you're not witty enough sober. But was the witty version of you just a babbling drunk, or is your normal self quite likable already? Explore these lies of alcohol logically. Soon enough, many crumble, replaced by a clearer sense of self. You might realize that alcohol never improved your jokes; it just made you laugh louder at them. Meanwhile, the rest of the room was politely tolerating you or equally intoxicated. That revelation alone can dissolve illusions about how entertaining alcohol makes you.

Another piece of the puzzle is to remain in the present. The lies of alcohol flourish by dragging you backward or forward. Past regrets can become monstrous if you dwell on them with alcohol as your only solution. Future worries can become mountainous if you fixate on them with the Evil Clown telling you that alcohol is your coping tool. The present moment, though, is seldom that dire. Right now, if you're reading this, you're presumably not mid-bender. You have clarity enough to read these words. In this moment, the Evil Clown can't force you to do anything. The question is whether you'll stay in the present or revert to alcohol's daydream the next time stress arises.

And about regrets—maybe you've already spent a chunk of life giving your intelligence away to delusions. That can sting. But the Evil Clown would like to spin that regret into more alcohol. Instead, view it as a wake-up call: better to see it now than never. Reclaim your intelligence and direct it toward building a better future, even if you only discovered the Evil Clown at 30, 50, or 70. The regret becomes a turning point, not a condemnation.

Consider that my entire fiasco on that plane might have turned into an actual business meltdown if I'd found a phone line. The Evil Clown almost coaxed me into emailing top professionals with that worthless idea. That's just one flight, one day of my drunken life. Multiply that by months or years, and you see how alcohol quietly degrades your judgment, sabotages your finances, and nudge you into unwise relationships or decisions. So is alcohol ever truly worth it, once you see behind the curtain?

If you feel a pang of sadness letting alcohol go, realize you're not losing genuine joy. You're losing illusions of joy that turned out to be fleeting and overshadowed by bigger costs. Freed from illusions, your real intelligence, your real sense of humor, your real capacity for relationship-building can blossom. Alcohol often dims the best parts of us while presenting itself as our helper, which is about as manipulative as it gets.

So if you're worried about missing out on that carefree euphoria alcohol sometimes provides, weigh it against the effects of alcohol that degrade your mental clarity. If you'd rather not risk writing meaningless business plans or sending bizarre texts at midnight, if you'd rather not see your kids or partner through a bleary lens, consider letting the lies you have told yourself go. Life on the sober side might not have that cheap, quick high, but it gives you something far more substantial: genuine clarity, real experiences, deep connections without alcohol's filter, and a sense of self you can trust not to vanish with the next bottle.

Chapter 5: Alcohol And Mental Health

Simon thought he had discovered the perfect shield for the low-grade hum of dread that stalked his rain-grey Tuesdays. A pint of lager, trailed swiftly by its identical twin, felt like bunking off school without getting caught. The corners of the world softened, the knot behind his sternum loosened, even the office printer looked philosophical beneath the strip-lights. Yet long after the bar stools were stacked, the shield turned traitor. At three in the morning he sat bolt upright, pulse racing as if he'd slept inside a bass drum, and wondered why a remedy could behave so much like a curse.

The potion we politely label "a drink" flicks two molecular switches that govern the emotional thermostat. GABA, the soft-spoken librarian, whispers "shhh" to excitable neurons, while glutamate, a caffeinated ringmaster, yells through a megaphone. The first swallow promotes GABA to head librarian and sends glutamate on gardening leave. Calm and confidence duly arrive, sometimes dragging karaoke along for the ride. Alas, the brain is an implacable accountant and detests unbalanced ledgers. Even before you locate the kebab shop it has printed a red-ink memo: reduce GABA, unleash glutamate. The wobble that follows is not a personal failing; it is homeostasis collecting its fee.

Those dawn palpitations feel intimate, yet the statistics insist they are tediously predictable. Regular drinkers are almost twice as likely to develop chronic anxiety, a dysfunctional romance in which each partner promises rescue and ends up nicking the other's wallet. Worse, every rescue attempt is self-defeating: to hush the rebound jitters people pour another measure, sharpening tomorrow's spike. It is rather like extinguishing a kitchen fire with petrol while telling yourself you have matters under steady control.

Pour dopamine into the mix and the plot thickens. That shy neurotransmitter normally demands novelty—sun on skin, a pay rise, a first kiss—before releasing its fizzy confetti. Alcohol jumps the queue, bribing the bouncer so dopamine showers us merely for lifting the glass. Over time the brain lowers its natural thermostat, waiting for ethanol before printing the party tickets. Day-to-day this translates into apathy, a flat mood, and the nagging suspicion that someone has drained the colour out of life and forgotten to mention it.

Depression is the sibling who gate-crashes this neurochemical jamboree. Longitudinal studies show heavy drinkers suffer roughly double the lifetime risk of major depressive episodes compared with light drinkers or abstainers. The relationship is causal, not coincidental: ethanol sabotages serotonin synthesis, erodes folate reserves, and shreds REM-sleep architecture—three nails in the coffin of mood stability. Fixing a leaking roof while drilling fresh holes would honestly be easier.

The sleep tale, though lacking the cinematic gore of liver failure, is pivotal. Alcohol chops down the time to nod-off, fooling every insomniac in the land. Yet passing-out is not sleeping; it is being walloped with a pharmaceutical mallet. Deep restorative cycles are truncated, REM sliced into ribbons, and the autonomic nervous system spends the night toggling between paralysis and panic. Wake up after drinking and the brain resembles a hardware store post-earthquake: everything technically present, nothing remotely where you left it.

Where mood darkens, risk follows. Suicide data drawn from decades and continents keep returning the same dejecting subplot: about half of completed suicides involve alcohol, and habitual drinking multiplies self-harm odds even after clinicians adjust for existing psychiatric labels. The drip-feed of disinhibition, impulsivity, and emotional volatility constructs a trap-door beneath moments of despair. By the time the glass is empty, choices have been signed off by a temporary board of disorganised neurons.

Many trauma survivors treat alcohol as an amateur therapist. The first beer hushes intrusive memories; the sixth grants amnesia's pardon. Unfortunately repeated chemical erasure prevents the hippocampus from filing those memories, and nightmares return sporting sharper teeth. Therapy is hard enough without pouring solvent over the archive.

But what happens when the tap is turned off? Contrary to melodramatic folklore, most drinkers do not collapse into eternal craving. Within a fortnight anxiety wanes, sleep improves, and mood climbs like ivy searching for sunlight. Cortisol falls, the pre-frontal cortex regains veto power over hare-brained schemes, and the gut microbiome—fussier than a Victorian dowager—throws fewer tantrums. Sobriety is less a moral crusade than a mechanical reset: unplug, wait, reboot, watch the crashes disappear.

None of this guarantees bliss. Old fears resurface, relationships need mending, Tuesday afternoons still turn sullen. Yet decisions are made in daylight rather than the yellow street-lamp glow of intoxication, and that alone tilts the odds. Problems people once tried to drown soon reveal a secret talent for swimming; drain the pool and they have nowhere left to lurk.

Seneca grumbled two millennia ago that drunkenness is "voluntary madness". Neuroscience merely colours-in the margins of his sketch. Alcohol's tranquillity tax accrues compound interest, payable in sleepless nights, bleak dawns, and the disquieting sense that one's personality has been rented out to strangers. Quitting often feels less like losing a pleasure and more like repossessing missing property.

Ask clients to picture life without booze and most imagine an endless beige corridor of denial. In reality, as the chemical fog thins they stumble upon forgotten doors: curiosity, resilience, mischief that doesn't end in tears. It is not saintly asceticism; more a factory-reset we were too inebriated to notice had been tampered with. Coaxing the brain to manufacture its own dopamine again takes patience, yet the dividends—authentic laughter, unscripted confidence—appear sooner than pessimists predict.

Persistent folklore claims a nip of something amber is the cheapest therapist in town. The evidence begs to differ. People who drink to "cope" are several times likelier to develop an anxiety disorder within three years than those who drink for taste or sociability. Coping drinkers fail to solve the original worries and accidentally hire alcohol dependence as a very expensive side-kick.

Hangxiety—an ugly portmanteau that ought to be plastered on bottles—deserves special mention. This hybrid of hangover and dread sprouts from the neuro-chemical see-saw set wobbling the night before. As glutamate gallops back into town, cortisol rallies the troops, and the amygdala starts sounding car alarms at passing clouds. Surveys report that almost half of people under thirty recognise this specific dread, proof that Mother Nature sends her invoices promptly.

Chronic drinking also rewires the stress apparatus. Once reserved for sabre-tooth tigers, the hypothalamic-pituitary-adrenal axis now ignites for the cork-screw. Elevated baseline cortisol correlates with depression and stunted neurogenesis in the hippocampus. Imagine driving permanently in second gear: loud, inefficient, and bound to break something expensive. Remove alcohol and the gearbox finally upshifts.

Another myth insists that alcohol quiets obsessive thinking by depressing the nervous system. Early relief is undeniable, much like silencing a smoke alarm with a hammer. Sadly, the hammer also smashes the sprinklers. Rebound excitation leaves the cortex more jittery than before, and compulsion loops tighten. Loss of inhibition pushes sufferers toward catastrophic expressions of their fears—checking, confessing, apologising—on a grander scale.

Alcohol's PR team goes further, portraying it as a creative muse. Yes, Hemingway edited life through a bottomless mojito, but he also ended life with a shotgun. Laboratory tests on divergent thinking, memory, and problem-solving record performance plunging after even moderate doses. Whatever brilliance the tipsy perceive is largely the illusion of ideas, not ideas themselves. A Dutch volunteer summarised the research neatly: "I composed a symphony last night, but it vanished with the pizza box."

Back to Simon. Two months dry, he discovers Tuesday is still grey but an ordinary grey, not the eldritch shade that hissed beneath the door at three a.m. He still sings karaoke; only now he remembers the lyrics and, mortifyingly, the audience cheering for an encore. His therapist no longer triages sessions around yesterday's drinking. The battered shield has been replaced by genuine armour: insight into his own unclouded emotions and the ability to act before calamity, not after.

Society, however, insists abstinence is unnatural. Politely declining a drink can trigger reactions normally reserved for refusing a parachute mid-skydive. Yet the cultural tide is turning. Alcohol-free bars are sprouting, mindfulness apps brag about sober streaks, and younger generations regard intoxication the way we view dial-up internet—quaint, noisy, weirdly slow. The drinker is no longer the life of the party; frequently he is the party's designated liability.

That shift matters because quitting alone is hard; quitting with stealth allies is simpler. Discover half the room ordered sparkling water, and willpower gets a free upgrade. Humans, bless us, copy whichever tribe seems happiest. Display the sober tribe laughing in full resolution, and the old slogans feel antique overnight.

One practical trick helps many novices: jot every unexpected perk of sobriety. Day ten: coffee tastes like coffee. Day twenty: woke up and felt good for the first time in a long time. Day thirty: dawn light on brickwork looks unreasonably dramatic. By day forty the handwriting shrinks to fit new gains. The exercise is childish on purpose; it drags the mind's spotlight off the minuscule list of losses and onto the stadium of benefits.

Relapses do occur. On edgy evenings I advise a ludicrously simple ritual: write the craving down, wait thirty minutes, then read it back. Desire is a diva; deny her an audience and she flounces off. Many are astonished when the monologue fades faster than an advert break. Will-power, it seems, thrives on delay.

After a hundred alcohol-free days Simon wanders into his old pub out of curiosity. He orders ginger-beer, chats to the staff, notices the same neon lights, the same Friday legends retelling stories they forgot they told last week. The nostalgia lasts nine minutes. He checks his watch, realises he can still catch the late film, and leaves with pockets full of money he once liquidated nightly.

The swap from anaesthesia to awareness forces an awkward question: What do you genuinely want to feel? Alcohol promises everything because desire is elastic. Remove the haze, and you discover the craving beneath the craving—connection, excitement, relief from boredom. None of these are solved by poisoning the liver; they are solved by living, sometimes messily, always awake.

O. Henry joked that civilisation is a race between education and catastrophe. In the matter of drinking, catastrophe is finally losing ground. We have the science, the stories, and the shifting culture. All that remains is today's decision to guard consciousness like a family heirloom. Make that choice once, then again tomorrow, and the days stitch together into something sturdier than will-power: a new identity.

Chapter 6: Alcohol – The Wolf Is In The Camp

Imagine an invisible puppeteer perched above every pub, wedding reception, corporate networking soirée and grief-washed wake, tugging at millions of strings in perfect unison. The marionettes—all of us—nod along to the clink-clink overture, raise glasses on cue, laugh a shade louder than the joke warrants, then shamble home convinced it was entirely their own idea. That puppeteer is ethanol, the garden-variety molecule that has spent centuries at finishing school, learning to pass as culture rather than chemistry. Cocaine, MDMA and their brisk cousins get hauled through the mud as 'drugs', but alcohol strolls past the bouncers with a cheeky wink, brandishing a fake passport marked Tradition.

How did we end up decorating newborns with champagne droplets while assuring ourselves we're fine role models? Biology helped. Fermentation is nature's accidental love letter to opportunists; fruit forgotten in the sun ferments on cue and our ancestors discovered that sipping the funky runoff made winter evenings warmer and saber-tooth encounters less existential. Genes that tolerated moderate intoxication without staggering into a sabre cat secured a tiny reproductive edge, so the taste for tipple embedded itself deep in the survival archive. Fast-forward twenty thousand harvests and Saturday night still feels incomplete without something that once lived as grape or grain.

History sharpened the hook. Medieval Europeans trusted ale more than water, not because they fancied a perpetual buzz but because water was often full of cholera and leeches. Brewers were the original public-health heroes, killing bacteria with boiling wort long before germ theory graduated from a twinkle in Pasteur's eye. Being a good parent meant giving your child "small beer" for breakfast. That generational endorsement remains etched on our collective hippocampus: beer equals safety and civilisation, even if today's municipal taps deliver water so pure it could cleanse a diamond.

Then came the marketing departments, the high priests of modern mythmaking. They studied our ancient craving for belonging and weaponised it into slogans. A bottled lager ceased to be fermented barley; it became camaraderie, machismo, beach volleyball, Christmas snow with carol singers in improbable knitwear. Wine labels drafted Bordeaux châteaux into romantic foot soldiers, implying that a Wednesday lasagna is a Tuscan sunset waiting to happen if only you pull this particular cork. Spirits took the brazen route—gin draped itself in art-deco misery chic, vodka masqueraded as liquid minimalism for the upwardly sleek. When governments finally slapped health warnings on packets of cigarettes, brewers slipped through the loophole, reminding legislators that nobody lights up a funeral or, heaven forbid, a christening, but a glass of fizz is practically compulsory.

Language plays the joker. We "have a drink," not "administer a central-nervous-system depressant." A "nightcap" sounds like a cosy item you might embroider, not a GABA-modulating sedative with a side order of REM sabotage. The English lexicon offers more synonyms for being drunk than Inuit allegedly have for snow, yet each synonym dilutes the seriousness: sloshed, plastered, merry, tipsy—all cartoon-friendly, none clinical. Nobody says., "I experienced acute ethanol poisoning last night," They admit sheepishly to being a bit "rough around the edges." Euphemism is the magician's cloak; hide the hand, reveal only glitter.

Social rituals cement the illusion. Toasts elevate alcohol to sacrament; the absence of a raised glass when someone retires feels heretical. Imagine responding to a wedding best man's "Charge your glasses!" by lifting a mug of camomile tea—everyone would assume you are either pregnant, pious, or deeply unwell. We label this peer pressure, but it is gentler than that, more like atmospheric pressure:

impossible to dodge unless you vacate the planet. It presses in soft, constant, persuasive. Even toddlers role-play with pretend tea sets, practising the choreography of convivial inebriation long before they can spell it.

Economics, of course, tucks quietly into the background with a calculator. Globally, alcohol revenue dwarfs the GDP of small nations. Governments, loath to slaughter such a cash-cow, settle for performative tut-tutting through advertising restrictions and token sin taxes. A politician wagging a finger at bourbon while pocketing millions in duty is akin to the fox convening a task force on hen-house security. So the state becomes an enabler, the stern parent who sells cigarettes out of the top cupboard while lecturing on lung health.

Science complicates the drama. Ethanol is water-soluble, seeps across the blood-brain barrier faster than gossip crosses a school playground. Once inside, it cosies up to those hardworking GABA receptors, whispering "Shhh, stop firing, relax," while simultaneously tickling glutamate into submission. The result is the familiar elevator: nerves slump, anxieties take a smoke break, self-censorship melts like ice in Mojito. That neurochemical lullaby feels fantastically medicinal to humans wrestling deadlines, heartbreak or Monday. It is also exquisitely temporary, which explains why the second glass looks heroic and the third inevitable. By dawn the pendulum swings the other way—glutamate rebounds, cortisol cackles, dehydration squeezes cerebral tissue like over-ripe fruit, and we promise the ceiling we'll never do it again. By lunch the puppeteer has retied the strings.

If this were cocaine, the warnings would be taught in kindergarten. Cocaine doesn't hide; it arrives with roving eyes and decibel-level confidence. Alcohol packages its threat in velvet. A tumbler on a mahogany shelf garnished with citrus peel looks positively statesmanlike. Even the scent is nostalgic—oak, vanilla, faint fireplace smoke. Try getting sentimental over the smell of petrol-cut methamphetamine.

To grasp how utterly normalised drinking has become, attempt a month-long abstinence and count the number of times someone worries for your wellbeing. "Everything okay?" "Have you had bad news?" "Are you on antibiotics?" Apparently sobriety needs a note from the doctor, whereas chronic intoxication requires only a karaoke machine and a taxi home.

I once attended a London networking event where the bar opened at 11 a.m. Start-up founders pitched seed-round visions while nursing artisanal IPAs, each brew boasting hops massaged by Tibetan monks. These are the same innovators building autonomous vehicles to save lives, yet none queried whether day-drinking might scramble the very neurons coding their breakthroughs. The disconnect would be comedic if it weren't tragic.

Acknowledging the deception is stage one of escape. When we label alcohol "just a social lubricant," we perpetuate the myth that the discomfort of sober conversation is intrinsic and immutable. It isn't. Social awkwardness is a toddler that grows into a monster only when fed fermented sugar. Leave it unfed, and it shrinks, replaced by genuine rapport. Real humour glitters sharper in the absence of slurred timing; authenticity rings louder when vocal cords aren't marinated in merlot.

Quitting is easier than you think precisely because the difficulty has been wildly overstated, mostly by people selling the stuff. Advertisements show omnipresent laughter because dull, repetitive evenings don't shift units. Marketing men know fear of missing out is a stronger sedative than the product itself. They curate montages where nobody vomits in a bush, nobody wakes at 3 a.m. with dread chewing their thorax, nobody sends a three-paragraph apology text riddled with baffled emojis. They never film the second half of the party when mascara resembles contemporary art and the host's Persian rug endures its annual white-wine baptism. Remove the montage, study reality, and the urge wilts.

Integration into Western life was never a sneaky corporate plot alone; we were enthusiastic collaborators. We craved shortcuts to confidence, community, creativity. Alcohol obliged, though each loan came with unpublicised interest. We drank for solidarity during war rationing, for bonhomie at peace treaties, for stamina during industrial revolutions. The very soldiers who returned from trenches with shellshock were issued "a tot" to soften nightmares, knitting trauma tighter rather than unravelling it. Generations later, their grand-kids toast Instagram follower milestones with prosecco and a Boomerang filter, unaware they are repeating the same chemically choreographed ritual, just in higher resolution.

There is irony too delicious to ignore: the more alcohol positions itself as a rite of passage, the more powerful the rebel who declines becomes. A teetotal teenager today exudes counter-culture mojo rivaling any punk rocker from 1977. They have decoded the con a full decade earlier than most of us; they will stride into adulthood with hangover-free mornings and bank accounts unpillaged by "just one more round." Meanwhile the rebels of old, clutch craft gin with botanical notes and sigh how the youth have changed.

But integration can unravel quicker than it knitted together. Observe the grassroots shift: sober-curious pop-up bars in Brooklyn, alcohol-free gin distilleries in Cornwall, mindfulness retreats where kombucha is the wildest thing on tap. Social media influencers post neon smoothies and hashtag #HangoverWho. Society is staging a quiet coup against its chemical overlord, starting not with prohibition sloganeering but with inviting alternatives that taste of possibility rather than penance.

The side effect is unexpectedly delightful. Remove alcohol from a dinner party and conversation sluices into new tributaries; no one repeats anecdotes because memory hasn't face-planted. Jokes stand on wit instead of volume. Dessert arrives and suddenly people notice flavours; apparently tiramisu has nuances masked for decades by cheap Chianti. The evening ends when energy dips, not when someone calculates how many units remain in the bottle. You wake remembering every detail, which might sound risky if your friends are tedious, but sobriety tends to upgrade one's friends as ruthlessly as it edited out the booze.

There will always be hold-outs prophesying gloom. They argue that a dry society is beige, sterile, soulless—that without alcohol Woodstock would have been a village fete with sensible footwear. Nonsense. Creativity thrived long before distilleries industrialised joy. Beethoven composed stone-cold sober symphonies; Jane Austen penned razor comedy on nothing stronger than tea. Laughing gas parties of the 1800s prove humanity will invent merriment from any molecule, yet none became as universal, or as quietly corrosive, as ethanol. Unplugging it simply shifts us back to default settings where pleasure emerges from context, not chemistry.

I once stood on a Mediterranean beach at sunset—yes, cue cliché violin—and noted couples raising beers to the tangerine sky. My hands circled a bottle of sparkling water. The scene felt no less spectacular; the colour wheel did not glitch because I lacked 5 percent ABV. In fact, I remember every contour of that horizon because synapses were busy recording, not slouching. Reality, unfiltered, is high-definition beyond any craft brew's promise.

Perhaps the greatest trick alcohol pulled was persuading us its absence will be noticed, remarked upon, judged. It really won't. People are far too absorbed in their own self-narratives to audit your glass. On the rare occasion they do, a shrug usually suffices. "I'm good with water tonight." Curiosity fizzles, conversation pivots to weather forecasts or cryptocurrency calamities. You are not the lead in their drama. Realising this delivers a jolt of liberty no cocktail could engineer.

If you still wobble, borrow a tactic from Stoic philosophers: memento mori. Visualise your tombstone. Below the elegantly carved name, imagine the epitaph: "He excelled at opening bottles." Unimpressive. Now picture an alternative inscription: "She met life with clarity." In the ledger of existence, clarity trumps claret. And you needn't forsake conviviality; the world teems with sober mischief—midnight hikes, salsa lessons that won't sprain ankles, board-game tournaments where 'Risk' is strategic, not hepatic.

Alcohol integrated itself so fully into Western life because we opened every gate, polished the hinges, and sold tickets at the door. The eviction notice therefore must come from us. Fortunately, the moment we stop paying rent, it packs its bags with startling speed. Three hangover-free dawns feel like new lungs; a fortnight reignites REM sleep so vivid you wake giggling at your own dreams; a month clears skin and bank statements. Ninety days and neurotransmitters re-learn to party unaided. Integration collapses like a sandcastle at high tide—magnificent in memory, absurd in retrospect.

By the time you read this, you may still believe you're fighting a giant. You're not. The puppeteer's strings are dental floss; one decisive snip and marionettes discover ankles. Western culture isn't a monolith; it's a kaleidoscope, forever one tilt from a brighter pattern. Remove the bottle and watch the shards rearrange into something sparklier and infinitely more stable. The secret hiding in plain sight is that you graduate from spectator to architect when you decline the illusion. And any architect will confirm: designing the party beats cleaning up after it.

Chapter 7: Antonis's Trip To Hell

Head's up! I am going to share a shocking story with you. This story is completely true, and I have neither changed nor embellished anything. Here in Cyprus, I have a friend called Antonis, or Tony as he is more commonly called. Tony and I were wardmates, which I admit sounds like we were locked up in the same mental facility together. However, it's not quite as exotic as that. On Sunday 27th April 2025, I woke with a sore stomach, nothing dramatic, I would say the pain was around three out of ten, but persistently there. I rode a bike with my friend Andrew, and the pain increased to a steady four. I spent a little time on FaceTime with my daughter, complaining about my stomach ache like a big baby, before my wife said lunch was ready. We sat and ate a tuna salad together, and pretty rapidly afterward, the pain decided to ramp things up a few notches. By mid-afternoon, it was so intense that I sat rocking in a chair, unable to do anything else. Eventually, I could take it no more and went to the local emergency room. I was ushered to the head of a pretty sizable queue and triaged as an urgent case.

Within an hour, I had been dosed up on morphine, x-rayed, and given a CT Scan before the senior doctor reported that I had appendicitis and needed emergency surgery. He said this while passing a medical disclaimer for me to sign; there was no time for debate. What followed was one of the worst experiences of my life, and one in which I believe I came very close to not making it. The hospital left me sitting in a corridor for so long that by the time the operation got started my appendix was in a state of being gangrene and had burst, flooding my abdomen with poison. The amount of pain and distress I went through over the next few days could fill a chapter. I could write a very graphic and exciting story of how I came close to meeting my maker but pulled through in the end. I am not going to do that because, no matter how creatively I wrote, my story would pail into insignificance when compared to the guy I shared a hospital room with during my stay.

Tony is a self-made man who decided to buy some farmland forty years ago and plant olive trees, perfect and resilient for this Greek island's harsh and hot environment. He would sell the olives to local suppliers and restaurants and every time he had a good year and a little extra in the savings account, he would buy more cheap land and repeat the process. Fast forward to 2025 and his entire family, including his daughter and two sons, work on the farm that has become the biggest in Cyprus. He owns 30,000 olive trees and 10,000 grape vines. This part of Cyprus is not significant for making wine, that is better done in the hills and mountain ranges, but the grapes are perfect for creating a powerful local spirit called Zivania. Ouzo is the national drink of Greece, but Zivania is the famous strong spirit of Cyprus, and it's absolutely revolting – but opinions may vary. Antonis is a large, rotund man with a vast and likable personality. Unfortunately, he has not only spent the last forty years making moonshine, but he's also spent a good percentage of that time drinking it. At sixty years old, his body is a trainwreck; he has prostate cancer, cirrhosis, and kidney failure. The doctors treat him as though a cure is still possible, but there is an elephant in the room that nobody wants to talk about. I think Tony knows that he has passed the event horizon; there is no way back from this level of damage. This affable and successful family man is on a railway track with only one destination left. Every night, at visiting time, his family would gather en masse, they would cry and comfort him, they would ask for the latest updates on his treatment, but at no point would anyone dare to mention or even look at the elephant in the room. It was as though, if nobody mentioned that he was dying, then it could not be true.

A few days after my admission, I was in a great deal of pain and discomfort because the severe infection was still threatening to overwhelm my system. Tony and I lay in our hospital beds, quietly moaning and grumbling to ourselves. He also had good reason to be feeling miserable; he was scheduled for surgery the following day to remove his cancer-riddled prostate. He had explained in graphic detail how it would be done, and even the thought of it filled me with pure terror. It sounded barbaric. Neither of us slept much that night. At 8 am, the porters arrived to take Tony down to the operating theatre, I wished him luck as he nervously shuffled onto the gurney. He was gone so long that I started to worry that something had gone wrong. Eventually, many hours beyond when he was due to return, the ward doors slammed open, and Tony was wheeled back in. He looked dead, indeed unconscious. His face was grey and there seemed to be no sign of life. Perhaps an hour or so passed with no movement or sound coming from his hospital bed. I was too scared to talk to him in case I disturbed him or somehow made his pain worse by bringing him back to reality. Eventually, when it was nearing midnight and the ward lights had been dimmed I heard a small, low croaky voice speak 'Craig', it said. I answered and only silence followed. I waited, not wanting to rush him or put any pressure on him. Eventually, he whispered, 'Something bad happened, something went very wrong, my friend'. What he went on to describe is the stuff of your worst nightmares.

Tony had been injected with propofol – the most commonly used general anaesthetic. Once he was confirmed to be unconscious, he was injected with a paralyzing agent that prevented any of his muscles from moving, not even a few millimetres. This of course, includes his lungs, so a breathing tube was inserted down his throat so machines could breathe for him. All, pretty standard practice for a surgical procedure of this magnitude. The problem was, Tony was awake, his eyes were closed, and his body motionless, but he was acutely aware of what was happening. He told me he could hear the surgeons talking, the radio playing, and the clatter of metal instruments. Desperately, he tried to scream, to move a limb, to do anything to alert the medical team that he was not unconscious, only paralyzed. I think you know what is coming next, and yes, it was every bit as horrendous as you can imagine. The surgeon began cutting into Tony between the anus and his genitals. He was awake, he was aware, he was entirely able to feel and experience the agony of being operated on. The experience lasted a few minutes; perhaps the medical team noticed distress in this heart rhythm, and more of the drug was injected. Tony awoke in the recovery room, not in a quiet, post-sedation bliss but screaming and in the middle of a full-blown panic attack. Truly the stuff of nightmares.

You probably have a few thoughts:

1.   Is this really possible?
2.   Why does it happen?
3.   How do I stop it from happening to me?

All thoughts I had myself and immediately asked Dr Google, who, apart from always telling me I am about to die, confirmed anaesthetic awareness is a rare and very traumatic complication that affects specific individuals. The primary catalysts for this surgical challenge are medication interactions and heavy alcohol and drug use. Yes, you heard me correctly. If you develop a sufficient tolerance to alcohol, it can translate into a tolerance to local and general anesthetics. I don't know about you, but that fresh hell is enough knowledge I need never to touch another drop of this evil poison.

Tony's terror didn't materialise out of thin air; it was incubated over the years in the repeated glasses of his favourite Zivania. Repeatedly bathing the brain in alcohol teaches it that inhibition is optional and that the GABA-A receptors—those microscopic bouncers that normally usher noise out of consciousness—should toughen up. They sprout extra sub-units, change shape, become the neurological equivalent of a nightclub doorman with a cauliflower ear. At the same time, the more excitable glutamate system, muzzled nightly by liquor, compensates by turning up the volume. The result is a neural orchestra forever practising fortissimo, and it takes a bigger pharmacological conductor to make them play pianissimo. Propofol is exquisite at that job in the average teetotaller, yet in a veteran drinker its baton can look suspiciously like a cocktail stick.

To make matters messier, the liver gets dragged into the conspiracy. Chronic drinking inducts cytochrome enzymes until they resemble a production line on Black Friday. Anything lipophilic that wanders into the hepatocyte is dismantled and shipped out quicker than you can say haemoglobin. Propofol is lipophilic royalty. So while the anaesthetist believes the syringe has delivered enough hypnotic to tranquillise a rhino, Tony's liver cheerfully hoovers up the payload and renders it about as effective as a soggy paper dart. This induces the sort of pharmacokinetic plot twist no one needs when scalpels loom.

Modern theatre kit is clever, but it still has blind spots. Heart-rate monitors notice panic only after the sympathetic nervous system storms the barricades; blood-pressure cuffs report mutiny every three minutes; EEG-based depth devices can misread the fireworks of alcohol tolerance as perfectly acceptable sleep. Meanwhile, paralysis drugs have done their mute-button magic, so the patient is trapped in a body that refuses to whistle for help. Awareness slips in through the side-door like an uninvited wedding guest, and by the time the clinical team recognises the gate-crasher, the damage has already drafted itself into long-term memory.

Curious about what had happened to Tony, I chatted with a consultant who compared anaesthetising a heavy drinker to "painting gloss onto wet oil." You add layers, yet it never quite dries. Pour on more, and the surface runs. Anaesthesia, like sobriety, works best when it doesn't have to wrestle your biochemistry. For years we convinced ourselves that a stiff nightcap helped us sleep; in truth, it merely stunned the cortex and left REM handcuffed in a cupboard. Now the pay-back arrives in theatre, where stunning the cortex is precisely the aim, except the dose-response curve is warped like a fun-house mirror.

If the body's defensive adaptations were limited to receptor tweaks and enzyme rallies, perhaps we could simply double the induction agent and move on. Alas, the cardiovascular system has its own subplot. Regular ethanol thins the autonomic brake pads; circulation that tolerated a pint of bitter without a tremor may buckle when faced with a scaled-up bolus of propofol. High doses can collapse blood pressure faster than a politician abandons a campaign promise, and hefty fluid resuscitation is not a hobby surgeons particularly enjoy. Thus the anaesthetist dances on a seesaw: too little hypnotic and Tony meets his nightmare, too much and the blood drains from vital organs like marbles through a colander.

Lurking behind the curtain is another villain—withdrawal. Suppose the patient, brimming with earnest good intentions, goes cold turkey forty-eight hours before admission. The pre-operative nurse smiles, ticks non-smoker, and writes "No ETOH since Monday." On the table, midway through a laparotomy, a hurricane of catecholamines blows in, blood pressure skyrockets, and the monitor draws arrhythmic hieroglyphs. Delirium tremens has a lousy sense of timing, and even a fully functioning dose of anaesthetic cannot drown every surge of noradrenaline. Recovery staff are left to corral a hallucinating, tachycardic elephant that none of the textbooks like to mention.

Transparency, then, is the first sedative. When the anaesthetist asks how much you drink, they're not performing a polite survey for an ONS spreadsheet; they're scouting for landmines. Handing them the unflattering truth may feel like confessing a double life, but it grants them the chance to load the toolbox with benzodiazepines, beta-blockers, extra monitoring and—should things drift— crisis algorithms honed on more simulations than Netflix has rom-coms. Conceal the numbers and everyone enters the theatre armed with guesswork and crossed fingers, never a reassuring combination.

Imagine, instead, the alternative timeline. Six months earlier you made the unremarkable yet seismic decision to become a non-drinker. Receptor expression began its slow waltz back to normality; the hepatic enzyme factory cut down its overtime; your REM sleep crept out of the cupboard, blinking, and got back to sweeping the cognitive workshop. By surgery day the anaesthetic nurse calculates the dose, presses the plunger, and—lo and behold—the drug behaves precisely as described in the pharmacology handbook. You fade out under lights so bright they could grow tomatoes, wake with a sore throat from the tube but no poltergeists clawing at the memory banks. The morphine PCA button feels decadent in its simplicity; you press it twice, daydream about dinner, and drift into the first genuine nap in years.

People sometimes query whether switching to wine spritzers or lengthening the gap between binges will spare them Tony's fate. Sadly, anaesthetic awareness cares little for the vintage and even less for the intervals. What counts is cumulative exposure—the relentless drip that teaches the brain to dodge bullets until it practically audition's for The Matrix. Tolerance is an uncannily efficient tutor; every session trains the synapse, every morning-after rewards compliance with another day's craving. Only abstinence hands neural circuits the study-leave they require to forget their bad habits.

There are myths worth smashing with a mallet. One claims that because alcohol is a depressant, it 'adds' to the sedative qualities of anaesthesia, meaning less drug will be needed. In acute intoxication that can hold true, though surgeons are understandably reluctant to slice into someone whose breath could ignite a petrol pump. Chronic intake flips the equation on its head. The body, ever resourceful, wages chemical warfare by upgrading its detox battalions. Those battalions do not clock off when anaesthesia starts; they treat propofol, etomidate, isoflurane and friends as just another round of bar-night chasers and throw them out before their job is done.

Another myth: a "few weeks off" is sufficient reset. It helps, certainly, but receptor numbers swing back according to biological calendars, not diary wishes. Three months buys noticeable normalisation; six months places you in the same pharmacological postcode as someone whose most daring beverage is peppermint tea. Dramatic? Yes. Impossible? Not even slightly. The organ with the greatest plasticity sits inside your skull, and it remodels faster than a property developer spotting cheap marble.

Perhaps none of this techy neurochemistry grabs you. Fair. Try the angle of dignity instead. Waking on a stretcher weeping from unspeakable memory fragments is indignity of the highest order. Taking steps today to prevent that tomorrow is an act of self-respect, not self-denial. Marcus Aurelius wrote that "the impediment to action advances action. What stands in the way becomes the way." Your impediment might be two bottles of Shiraz each night. Remove it, and the path flings itself open—not only toward uneventful surgery but toward sharper mornings, conversations recalled in full, cheeks no longer puffed from hidden inflammation, and the curious discovery that supermarket aisles are wider when you're not darting past the wine rack.

If alcohol has been your loyal, corrosive companion for decades, the prospect of quitting can look like preparing for life on Mars. That's fine; you needn't sign a fifty-year contract this evening. Promise yourself today plus twenty-four hours. If that feels achievable, collect another twenty-four. Brain chemistry will notice, trust me. Tolerance has an ego but it also has amnesia; starve it of reinforcement and it forgets quicker than a toddler flings peas. One dawn, you'll hear your alarm and realise the night passed without duvet wrestling, sweats or the bleak echo of 3 a.m. despair, and you'll smile—the small, private smile of a person whose inner auditorium no longer demands constant sedation.

Quitting drinking is easier than you think not because the journey lacks potholes but because the destination removes so many hidden tolls. Tony paid in terror, yet gave the rest of us a visceral reminder of what's really at stake. You, dear reader, can pay nothing more than the price of your next round getting left on the bar. That feels like a bargain even to my thrifty Yorkshire soul.

Chapter 8: Lie Down with Dogs – Get Up with Fleas

It's astonishing how heavily the Western model of success is intertwined with alcohol, to the point where owning a luxurious home seems incomplete without a well-stocked wine cellar. Anyone daring to buck that trend and reject the siren call of merlot or champagne inevitably finds themselves battling more than personal cravings. They're grappling with the collective spell that insists fine wines are part and parcel of living the good life. If you doubt that claim, think about the media frenzy that erupts whenever well-heeled bankers spend tens of thousands of dollars on a single meal's worth of "rare vintage" plonk. Some spectators applaud the extravagance, as if it indicates refined taste. Others are offended by the excess but rarely question the deeper assumption lurking underneath: that expensive alcohol is a status symbol we should aspire to.

The marketing machine behind booze is infinitely more cunning than the old campaigns for cigarettes. Tobacco might have once been pitched as glamorous, but society eventually turned on it. Alcohol, on the other hand, gets away with far more because it hides behind a veneer of sophistication and "health benefits." The industry is brilliant at feeding the notion that certain bottles will elevate your standing in life. Once you swallow that message, you can be manipulated into seeing yourself as inadequate unless you too can produce a top-dollar champagne at your next dinner party. The underlying logic that you're being conned by an expensive poison rarely comes to the surface.

Champagne stands out as one of the more absurd examples of this snobbery. Essentially, it's just sparkling white wine from a region of France that seems to grow wider every time they redefine its borders. It's sold everywhere, from supermarket shelves at twenty bucks a pop to boutique wine merchants with four-figure price tags. And that's not even the end of it. There's an entire ecosystem of brand prestige within the world of champagne. A thirty-dollar bottle might be turned away by so-called connoisseurs, who demand a pricey Cristal or Krug instead. At media events or high-society galas, some people literally won't touch anything else. They posture as cultured or discerning, when all they're really doing is paying a premium for a marketing fable so potent it might put the Pied Piper to shame.

One way to understand how these lies gain so much momentum is to appreciate two of the strongest motivating forces in human psychology: scarcity and social proof. Scarcity, by definition, inflates value. Diamonds cost a fortune largely because of their perceived rarity, and even though we can debate how controlled that supply might be, the mere suggestion that something is in short supply makes the price skyrocket. Fine art, antiques, limited-edition sneakers—it doesn't matter. If it's scarce, it grows more desirable. Alcohol producers use exactly this principle when they portray certain bottles as "exclusive," with limited runs, fancy packaging, or references to special terroir. People chase the notion of being special, and brand snobbery thrives on that.

Then there's social proof, the principle that if many people do (or believe) something, there must be a good reason. Decades ago, psychologists Milgram, Bickman, and Berkowitz famously had a handful of people stand on a street corner, looking up at the sky. If one person stood there staring, a few passersby might glance up. If five did it together, more folks would stop. Ramping up the numbers made it increasingly likely that random people would crane their necks at the empty sky, convinced something up there must be worth seeing. With drinking, you get a similar effect: the majority of society raises a glass, so we assume it's a logical, perhaps even beneficial, habit to adopt. Rarely do people think, "Wait, is everyone just staring at nothing in the sky?" They simply assume that if so many folks are partaking in booze, it must be fine.

When nearly everyone around you is sipping something at the bar, it creates a silent pressure to join in. If you dare to say no, people often become uneasy or defensive. It's not that they're threatened by your refusal itself. Rather, you're shining a light on the possibility that what they're doing may not be so wise after all. Nobody likes being confronted with that uncomfortable truth. If you've ever walked into a pub and asked for water or soda, you'll notice that look of bewilderment crossing people's faces. Sometimes they get almost apologetic, in that tone of, "I'm so sorry you can't drink—are you driving? Are you ill?" If you say, "No, I just don't want alcohol," it's as though you've insulted them personally. There's a reason for that dynamic, and it's rooted in our innate desire to avoid pain.

People subconsciously realize alcohol is harmful. The signs are hard to miss: hangovers, regrets, embarrassing photos from last night's revelry. Despite that, they cling to the routine because they perceive more comfort than danger. But the moment you stand in front of them, stone-cold sober by choice, you highlight the fact that there's another route. That your approach reveals something about their own reliance on the drug can cause them psychological discomfort. In response, many will try to coax you back into the fold so they don't have to question their own choices.

It's the classic scenario: you politely decline a glass, and someone exclaims, "Oh, come on, don't be such a buzzkill." Or they say, "One little drink won't hurt," and grin at you like you're a party-pooper for refusing. This reaction is simply them seeking relief from the guilt or discomfort triggered by your refusal. If you continue to say no, they're forced to look inward, and they'd rather not do that. So it's easier to chide you for being a stick-in-the-mud than acknowledge the illusions they've bought into.

This environment makes it incredibly tough to rely on willpower alone to quit. Even if you manage to push down your own cravings, you're bombarded by external triggers: friends pressing drinks on you, society praising expensive wines as symbols of success, ads claiming moderate consumption has health benefits. Nobody tries to sabotage you from giving up cigarettes with that much fervor, because cigarettes have largely lost their social luster. Meanwhile, alcohol is so embedded in our celebrations, commiserations, and daily unwinding rituals that you're forever paddling against the tide.

And it's not just the people in your immediate circle. It's the entire cultural backdrop. We'll see headlines about this or that billionaire's favorite rare cognac, or read magazine articles that treat "cellar selection" like the hallmark of refined living. The message is persistent: If you want to be part of the elite, you need an appreciation for these pricey toxins. Over time, you might even buy into it unconsciously, half-believing that stepping away from alcohol is stepping away from what's normal, adult, or sophisticated.

In reality, you're stepping away from a contrived story, not from genuine adulthood or refined taste. Yet the beliefs are so strong, they bleed into every aspect of social life. You can see it in how quick people are to question you if you turn down free booze. Nobody hunts you down in the same manner if you decline, say, free peanuts. Only when it's about drinking does someone frown at you like you've broken an unwritten rule. The so-called "etiquette" of drinking can be downright bizarre. An example might be a flight attendant who feels disappointed when you politely order juice instead of wine, as though refusing free liquor is a personal affront. In a society that normalizes near-compulsory drinking, your abstinence can appear offensive or suspicious.

It's almost comical to imagine if the same dynamic applied to something else. Suppose you go to a party where people are passing around lumps of raw jalapeño peppers. They're devouring them, eyes streaming with tears, proclaiming how it's the only way to have a good night. If you say "No thanks, I'm good," they respond, "You sure? You don't know what you're missing, it's amazing." That doesn't happen in real life because the group doesn't need you to partake in the pepper to validate their own behavior. With alcohol, though, the illusions run deeper.

Part of the reason alcohol has such a tight grip is our innate drive to be included, to feel that we're part of a group. This is exactly where social proof becomes powerful. If you're the only one in a crowd not raising a glass, your primal instincts ping an alert: Are you jeopardizing your acceptance in the group? Are you risking potential ostracism? That fear can override logical thinking. The easiest, laziest path to belonging is to pick up a glass and cling it with everyone else, no questions asked.

Most of the people pressuring you to drink are themselves slaves to illusions. They're busy ignoring the fact that alcohol is a poison they've come to crave. Some are deeper into the trap than others, yet they all cling to it for the same fundamental reasons: the need to avoid pain and gain pleasure, the desire for social acceptance, or sometimes simply the force of habit. So it's not that your friend (or random bar acquaintance) wants you to fail at sobriety out of malice. They probably love you just fine. But deep down, they'd rather not see you succeed in stepping away from the drug, because it would raise uncomfortable questions about their own choices.

When the majority of people in your life are still in the clutches of alcohol, how do you stand firm? First, you have to stop explaining or justifying yourself. The more you try to defend your decision to go sober, the more pushback you'll get. Trying to convert them to your viewpoint can be an exercise in futility. Imagine standing in a hailstorm, shouting at the ice pellets to stop. They won't. Your best bet is to find an umbrella or move indoors. In the same way, you can shift your social interactions or seek out people who don't mind if you're not guzzling. If you keep hanging out exclusively in smoky bars or boozy dinner parties, you're choosing the hardest path, especially in the early days of sobriety.

It's a bit like trying to learn a foreign language for an hour a week, then going back to an environment where nobody else speaks that language. Progress is slow and stunted. But if you immerse yourself in a place where the new language is all around you, you pick it up with astonishing speed. Likewise, immersing yourself in an environment where sobriety is normalized can work wonders. Online communities, for instance, are a great resource; you can find groups of people with the same goals, exchanging stories, tips, or encouragement. This offset is crucial because you'll continue to face that social proof from the drinking world. Having a safe space where the illusions are recognized for what they are can provide the balance you need.

Of course, your old circle of friends might be baffled. They might see your improved health, sharper mind, and calmer presence and resent you for it, or pretend not to notice. That's not your responsibility. If you stand tall in your decision, some might eventually come around, sometimes out of curiosity or because they see your success and want a piece of that. Until then, you owe no one an explanation about "why you're not drinking." There's no need to claim you're on antibiotics or invent an early morning appointment that precludes alcohol. Doing so only perpetuates the notion that you must have an external "excuse." You don't. You simply don't want to ingest poison. That is explanation enough, even if it confounds or irritates them.

An odd phenomenon arises here: people often state they don't trust non-drinkers. Perhaps you've run into that attitude once or twice. A friend may half-joke, "I just can't trust a man who doesn't drink." On the surface, it sounds silly, but it's a product of deep conditioning. Society has hammered home that alcohol is integral to building camaraderie, letting your hair down, and showing your true self. If you skip the booze, you might be viewed with suspicion, as though you're hiding something or refusing to "join the team." This ironically flips reality upside down. We should be asking why so many feel the need to rely on a chemical crutch just to express themselves or connect with others.

The truth is, a sober person might be more trustworthy. At the very least, they're clearer in mind, less prone to impulsive outbursts, and more likely to remember what they agreed to do the next day. But that doesn't fit the narrative the marketing departments have spent decades seeding in our collective imagination. They would far rather keep you enthralled with visions of carefree laughter, scenic vineyards, or rare barrels that cost an arm and a leg. The less you question, the easier it is to keep you as a customer.

A particularly interesting scenario emerges in situations where alcohol is offered for free. The logic in polite society goes like this: you never turn down free booze. If you do, people look at you as though you've thrown a gift in their face. Some might genuinely be hurt, especially if they perceive your refusal as rejection of their hospitality. On an airplane, for instance, a flight attendant might push wine or whiskey on you to be kind, to make your experience special. If you politely refuse, they can't compute the idea that maybe you're just not interested in alcohol at 37,000 feet. They might start brainstorming reasons why you would say no: Maybe you're on medication, maybe you're driving after landing, maybe you're pregnant. The notion that you simply don't want to ingest ethanol is so foreign that they'll mentally rummage for any plausible justification but that.

That same surreal confusion can greet you at wedding receptions, corporate events, or barbecues. The host may wave you over with an enthusiastic grin, brandishing a glass. "Here, have a drink!" If you politely respond, "No thanks, I'm good," they often look crestfallen. You might almost hear them thinking, "What's wrong with you, my friend?" Or they scurry off to find a "better" beverage that might entice you. If you hold your ground, they eventually drift away, sometimes with a vague sense of unease. Then the rumor mill can begin: "I heard he doesn't drink. Wonder why…" If you're unlucky, they might spin theories about how you must be in recovery or how you're super religious or dealing with a dark secret. Rarely does anyone conclude, "He's probably just realized it's a poison and has no desire to ingest it." That doesn't compute with the lies.

Nevertheless, none of these scenarios are as bad as they might seem when you view them from a calm vantage point. Once you see the illusions, the social pressure to drink becomes more like background noise. It may still be irritating or awkward, but it doesn't derail your resolve. You recognize that the underlying tension for other people is the fear you might be right—fear that their dependence on alcohol is not quite as harmless or sophisticated as they pretend. Instead of letting that moment rope you back in, you can approach it with a little empathy. They're not attacking you personally; they're defending their illusions.

One approach is to simply smile, say, "No thanks," and move on. No big statements about being teetotal or living a grand sober life, no lectures on how alcohol kills thousands each year. That often triggers defensive responses, as though you're judging them. You can simply enjoy the party in your own right, sipping a non-alcoholic beverage, munching on snacks, or chatting about everyday topics. Over time, some might notice you're perfectly at ease without a drink in hand, which might intrigue them more effectively than any sermon on the perils of ethanol.

The question arises: can you maintain friendships with heavy drinkers once you go sober? Possibly yes, but the dynamic often shifts. If your entire friendship was built around hitting bars or wine-tasting events, it can be challenging to find common ground at first. True friends will adapt and accept that you're not drinking. They might still feel a bit unsettled at times, but genuine connections usually survive if the bond goes beyond shared intoxication. People who vanish from your life because you no longer partake in the bottle might have been acquaintances propped up by the drug culture, more than true companions.

You also might discover that you don't enjoy certain hangouts as much as you did when you were numbing yourself. That's normal. If the only reason you tolerated a certain bar or event was because you were plastered, now you might find it downright dull or irritating. That can be a sign that you never really liked it in the first place—the booze was just covering the boredom or distaste. So your social life might morph, but that's not necessarily a negative. It can free up time and energy to explore new hobbies or friendships that align with the sober version of you.

The mental shift away from "I can't have a drink" to "I don't need or want a drink" is crucial. If you frame it as deprivation, you'll feel the pinch of every social scenario. If you recognize it as liberation, you'll discover how nice it is to walk away from an evening with your wallet intact, no fuzzy memories, and zero regrets. The world's not going to bestow any medals on you for not drinking, obviously, but you might award one to yourself for reclaiming your autonomy from a drug that's so pervasive. Plus, as your circle sees you living a calm, productive life without hangovers, some might start to wonder if you're onto something. They might approach quietly, weeks or months later, asking, "How do you do it?"

You can explain it or choose not to. My suggestion is to show them how you live now—no regrets, no morning-after dread, no anxious rummaging for an excuse. If they're sincerely curious, you can gently talk about illusions, how you realized you'd been sold a scam from childhood, how you recognized it was just a trap disguised as social fun. If they're not receptive, that's fine too. You can't forcibly open someone's eyes to beliefs they're not ready to question. We all move at our own pace in life.

One helpful trick is to keep your sense of humor about the entire situation. Sometimes, this bizarre wonderland of clinking glasses and shared delusions can be so strange it's almost comical. You might see an entire group of people laughing uproariously at jokes that aren't particularly funny, stumbling around in new shoes that aren't even broken in yet, and bragging about how they're going to feel it tomorrow, as though that's an achievement. In your new vantage, you might watch with a combination of amusement and compassion. You remember when that was you. You also see that, at some point, they'll wonder why they keep repeating the cycle.

That's the environment you're up against. It's no wonder that using sheer willpower to refrain from drinking is like taking a plastic sword into battle. The pressure to conform is unrelenting, the lies about wine cellars and "top-shelf liquor" are hammered from every direction, and the social cues to raise a glass are nearly universal. But illusions can't survive serious scrutiny. Once you've dismantled them for yourself, they lose their power over you. The key is to dismantle them thoroughly, so that no matter how many friends raise a brow at your refusal, or how many free flutes of champagne come your way, you see the real product for what it is: a slow poison that's been cleverly disguised as an elite lifestyle accessory.

No single conversation with a pushy friend or confused flight attendant should ever be allowed to rattle your sense of peace. You're the one who has stepped out of the matrix. In a world that still has a faint whiff of delirium about this substance, you're the rarity—a mind unclouded by the group madness. That might cause some friction in the short term, but it also grants you an independence that's impossible to overstate.

So, you skip that glass, or you politely pass on the shot. Maybe an eyebrow is raised, a joke is made at your expense. No big deal. You can laugh it off. Meanwhile, you're enjoying the clarity of mind that comes from not playing a tug-of-war with your own impulses. You'll wake up feeling fresh, able to keep your day's plans without battling a hangover. Let the rest of the crowd call you boring. Boring is sometimes code for "immune to illusions." Let them come to their own conclusions. You have bigger things to do—living a vibrant, sober life in a culture that insists you need to be tipsy to be normal.

And if ever your confidence wobbles, just think of how bizarre it is that we treat people who reject an addictive poison as if they're the weird ones. That alone should remind you how deeply we've drunk from the communal Kool-Aid. In a sense, acknowledging the madness can be liberating. You realize you're not missing out on something wonderful; you're declining a culturally sanctioned alcohol. It might look fancy in crystal glasses or accompanied by sophisticated chatter about flavor notes, but it's alcohol all the same.

When you don't need alcohol to handle social situations, you discover which ones truly make you happy and which ones you merely tolerated because you were half-numb. You might refine your social circle, or keep it as is but approach your relationships more consciously. While some old acquaintances might drift away, the friends who remain often appreciate having a designated, fully present companion. They know you'll remember the stories they told, or the promise they asked you to keep. You can keep them safe if they overdo it, and ironically, you might become the stable anchor in a swirl of drunken chaos.

Ironically enough, it's not uncommon for people to express envy at your ability to remain clear-headed. They'll see you sipping on a soda and assume you have unbreakable self-control. Little do they realize that once illusions are gone, self-control is barely necessary. You simply aren't enticed. It's not about resisting. It's about not wanting something that has no real appeal once the illusions are stripped. That's the ultimate mental shift, and no amount of peer pressure or pitying looks can knock you off course once you reach that point.

So carry yourself with the assurance that you're the one seeing reality, and it's a far more fulfilling reality than the dream sold on TV or in wine magazines. Alcohol was never your friend, no matter how nicely it dressed up in marketing campaigns. Understand that most people defending it haven't yet peeled away the illusions. They cling to the "benefits" of being accepted by the group, the fleeting euphoria, the sweet sense of belonging. You, on the other hand, are free to belong on your own terms, forging deeper, more genuine connections without a chemical middleman. That's a powerful place to be.

When you next face that baffled flight attendant, or the hostess at a party who can't understand why you won't toast the evening with a potent beverage, remember you're not the one committing a social crime. You're the rational, sober-minded adult who sees the bigger picture. Let them cock their head in confusion. Let them call you dull or prissy. You get to walk away with your integrity intact, your health unscathed, and your wallet a bit thicker. That's not a sacrifice; that's a wise trade-off.

Chapter 9: Threshold

Pause for a moment and consider the forces that are at work, urging you to pick up a drink. It might seem like an innocuous moment: you get home from a busy day, your feet are sore, and there's a bottle of wine conveniently waiting in the cupboard. You believe that glass will soothe you, offer a bit of comfort or unwinding. Yet beneath that simple act, there's a complex web of motivations pulling the strings. If you examine them closely, you'll find they boil down to a pair of stubborn impulses: you crave pleasure and you try to avoid pain. Nothing more, nothing less. Everything you do, big or small, is connected to these two primal urges.

Imagine you decide to take a long look in the mirror. You might notice aspects of your physique you're less than thrilled about. Perhaps you feel self-conscious about your weight, or you wish you had the stamina to run up a flight of stairs without gasping for air. If these issues genuinely trouble you, you'd think the fix is straightforward: exercise more, adjust your diet, improve your habits. But countless people, perfectly aware they're unhappy with their body, never make the necessary changes. Why is it so common for human beings to tolerate a state they dislike rather than do whatever's needed to escape it?

The logic is harshly simple: People see more perceived "pain" in the process of transformation than they see pleasure in the end result. Sure, being slim or fit would be amazing. You might picture yourself wearing clothes that fit snugly in all the right places, stepping outside to appreciative glances from strangers who wonder if you're an athlete or a model. That scenario is quite appealing. But the path to get there—exercise, discipline, skipping indulgences—can feel daunting enough to overshadow the potential payoff. So they opt to remain stuck in that unsatisfying status quo, perpetually daydreaming about a better body without ever shifting their routine.

The parallel to drinking is glaring. You know, if you're honest, that life would be better without daily doses of a toxic depressant swirling around your bloodstream. Quitting would mean more disposable income, deeper, less disturbed sleep, sharper focus, and the reassurance that you're no longer dancing on the edge of a health crisis. So why not just stop? Well, because for most people, the pain they associate with parting ways with alcohol appears far bigger than the pleasure they anticipate from sobriety. Psychologically, it looks like a net negative, even though it's not.

And that's precisely why so many transformations never take off until something truly jarring happens—a threshold moment. This is the point at which the pain of continuing becomes so acute that it overwhelms any fear of change. Typically, it's triggered by a crisis that snaps you out of denial and forces you to look at the full damage you're inviting by not acting. Suddenly, the scale tips. The misery of staying the same outweighs your dread of the cure, and in that window, you might leap into action.

Maybe your threshold moment is your child drawing a picture of you slumped on the sofa, a bottle in hand. Children don't soften the edges; they depict what they see. You spot that cartoonish image they've proudly colored in, and it slices right through all your excuses. Suddenly you realize that, in your daughter's eyes, you've become the person permanently fused to a wine glass. Or you read a story from someone who grew up with an alcoholic parent and recall your own neglected child in the other room, the one you keep telling you'll play with "after just one more." In that raw flash of understanding, the agony intensifies, and you may decide it's time to do something—anything—to escape the path you're on.

People often gather threshold moments like stepping stones across a river: first, a spouse complains, then a boss subtly warns that your performance is slipping, then a grim health scare arrives. Each time, the pain shoots up a notch, and for a brief while you might put the bottle down, but if you're relying purely on willpower, your determination ebbs away once the panic subsides. If you never shift your deeper perception of alcohol from "something I like but can't have right now" to "something that's purely harmful," you get stuck in a cyclical trap.

That cyclical nature was painfully apparent in my own life. I used to be an exceptionally heavy drinker, though I resisted the word "alcoholic." I told myself alcoholics were those unkempt men in doorways, nursing cheap whiskey from a paper bag. I had a career and a family, so I couldn't possibly be that. Meanwhile, I was guzzling two bottles of wine a night, sometimes maneuvering events so I could smuggle whiskey into places that offered no booze. Strange how we can be so cunningly blind to our own predicament. The black-and-white lies we set up—"I'm not homeless, so I can't be an addict"—are part of how we dodge reality.

I even convinced myself that because I didn't crave a drink first thing in the morning, I didn't have a serious problem. But every day after work, I'd drop into a mental autopilot, reaching for the first bottle and draining half of it before dinner. By bedtime, two bottles would be gone, and I might lie awake, listening to my heart pound, telling myself I should slow down, all while refusing to accept the real scope of the problem. Tinkering around the edges—like throwing out a half-glass of wine so I could proclaim I hadn't actually had two bottles—became the norm.

This spiral continued until a threshold moment slammed into me like a freight train. It arrived in the shape of a nagging pain under my ribcage. At first, I explained it away—food poisoning, maybe a strange muscle spasm. But it wouldn't subside. Then came the internet searches, the horrifying possibilities of liver cirrhosis or pancreatic failure. It was no longer some vague risk I pushed to the back of my mind; it was immediate, personal, and terrifying.

When I eventually found myself in a doctor's office for a barrage of tests, the gravity sank in. A variety of scanning machines poked and prodded me, looking for the extent of the damage. I recall a day when I finally realized there was no polite way to ignore it: I was uncomfortably close to a future where my children might be left fatherless, my wife widowed, my life cut short because I chose to cling to a daily bottle. The emotional pain of that scenario for the first time outweighed the pain of imagining life without drinking. My threshold had arrived.

But, as with many people, I still tried to bargain with the craving. I set up "systems," like lockable cabinets. I'd try limiting myself to a single measure a night, trusting a spouse or friend to hold the key. In the moment, that sounded like a perfect solution. But then the first time that key-holder was out for the evening—and I "deserved" my daily measure—I discovered the cheap plywood backing of the cabinet could be jimmied open. No plan lasts long if at your core you still crave the substance like a lifeline. The moment the "pain impetus" fades, you fall back on old habits because you still view alcohol as beneficial deep down.

Interestingly, once I recognized that threshold moments spark dramatic short-term changes but rarely sustain them, I realized that real liberation lay in altering how I perceived alcohol altogether. If I kept seeing it as a guilty pleasure I was "denied," I'd remain stuck fighting internal battles. If, on the other hand, I taught myself to see that it was purely harmful—poison elegantly packaged—I might lose the desire to drink it in the first place.

This same dynamic is common for folks in other areas of life. If you're discontent with your job but dread the upheaval of looking for a new one, you might resign yourself to misery for years. Or if you hate your living situation but fear the cost and hassle of relocating, you might stay put indefinitely. People only move when the balance of pain tips the other way, or until they truly shift their perspective. With drinking, it's not enough to scold yourself or craft a half-baked plan to ration your intake. You have to realize the beliefs that keep you tethered to the glass—that it somehow tastes good, calms you, makes you sociable, or helps you sleep—are illusions, repeated so many times you eventually accepted them as fact.

Hearing from others who've walked this path can be eye-opening. One woman, Linda, wrote to me about growing up with an alcoholic mother. Her story is heartbreakingly raw: she felt neglected, unloved, overshadowed by the bottle her mom clutched so tightly. She saw how her mother used booze to cope with every stress or hardship. By the time Linda was a teenager, her model of "normal drinking" was basically drinking to unconsciousness, because that's what she'd observed. She recalled being mortified whenever her mother turned up drunk at school functions. Yet that was the environment she considered normal. Some kids replicate the same pattern in adulthood; others run from it in fear. But Linda ended up wrestling with her own destructive relationship to alcohol for a long time. The impact of an addicted parent can ripple through a child's entire life.

It's one thing to read Linda's words, feeling sympathetic. It's another to realize that your own child might be scribbling a crayon portrait of you with a beer can in your hand. Children watch everything, remember everything. If you keep endorsing a nightly ritual of alcohol, you're also endorsing that pattern for them. The myth that your kids "never see you drunk" doesn't necessarily spare them from the consequences. They sense more than you think. One day, that might be your threshold moment: the day your little boy or girl points out, with brutal honesty, the bottle you never put down.

But threshold moments can also be quiet. A midnight health scare, a friend's concerned expression when you're polishing off a bottle alone, or a burst of clarity as you wake with a monstrous hangover. The problem with threshold events is that they fade. Pain is acute but fleeting. Once it recedes, you're left relying on that old, rickety tool:

willpower. And if your mind still believes "I need booze to get through life," willpower is no match for your subconscious. Day by day, the internal tension wears you down, and inevitably you give in. That's how countless people vow every Monday to cut down, only to crack by Wednesday.

You see the same phenomenon in dieting. Someone stands in front of the mirror, deeply upset about their shape, so they vow to follow a strict diet. That vow holds until they realize they're starving, bored, or craving some sweet indulgence. The brain registers famine, goes into survival mode, and bombards the person with signals to eat. Most revert to old habits within days or weeks, sometimes ending up heavier than before. Willpower rarely solves an internal conflict.

In the context of alcohol, it's the conflict between "I should quit" and "I still want it." If you remain in that tug-of-war, any threshold moment will produce only a temporary victory. As soon as life calms down, the siren song returns, especially once you convince yourself it's safe to have "just one." So the real transformation—the path out of this maze—requires changing your fundamental picture of alcohol from something beneficial to something entirely worthless or harmful. That's not something you achieve through short bursts of willpower; it's a deeper re-education. Usually, it involves noticing that the taste isn't nearly as wonderful as your illusions have pretended, that the relaxation is artificial alcohol, that any perceived bravado or social ease is overshadowed by a thousand awkward or destructive outcomes.

Realizing that the illusions are precisely that—illusions—can be liberating. You start noticing the sweetness that's used to mask the poison. You remember that your very first sip of alcohol, as a kid, probably tasted awful and left you recoiling. If it's such a natural, delicious beverage, why did we have to force ourselves to get used to it? Why do we bury it under fruit juices, fizzy mixers, and sugary syrups? If you strip away the fancy packaging, the exotic naming conventions, and the illusions hammered into us by marketing, you're left with a chemical that kills germs on contact and damages organ cells. The journey is about bridging the gap between logically knowing that and believing it so deeply that you no longer feel deprived when you say no.

Consider the story of my threshold moment once the hospital visits started. For eight weeks, I quit. That intense fear was a rocket booster that overcame my usual excuses. Then, as the pain receded, I told myself, "Surely I can have just a glass now and then." The hospital had done its job of shocking me, but I still viewed alcohol as something pleasant I was missing. So I returned to the bottle, only to land back in the doctor's office with worsened symptoms soon after. My lies weren't shattered enough to keep me from creeping back.

That creeping-back scenario is the crux of so many unsuccessful attempts to cut down or moderate. People set elaborate rules: only on weekends, never before 7 p.m., only half a bottle. But if you consider alcohol a friend you can't wait to hang out with, your mind devotes its cunning energy to finding loopholes in your rules. Suppose you lock the liquor cabinet; you might find another stash or run to the store for more. Or you skip social events that won't serve alcohol. Or you pick the dinner invitation that ensures "wine is included," ignoring other more fulfilling family outings. That's the classic pattern of an enslaved mind, always seeking the next fix and calling it normal.

Think about the culture around you. Billions are spent on adverts showing glamorous people swirling wine in fancy glasses, claiming you can't fully enjoy a meal or party without a little "something to loosen up." Entire TV shows revolve around comedic or dramatic scenes of drunken escapades, as if every emotional reveal needs a wine glass in hand. We see these delusions so often that they become second nature. Your internal conversation might whisper, "It's not really a celebration without champagne." Or "I won't be relaxed after work unless I have that evening glass."

Those messages are a kind of corporate hypnosis. They embed themselves in your subconscious so that any attempt to quit triggers alarm bells: "But life won't be the same, how will I unwind?"

Yet if you step back, you see how contradictory this is. We started talking about how everything in life revolves around chasing pleasure and avoiding pain. If you truly believed alcohol brought more pain—lost days from hangovers, emotional breakdowns, financial holes, health nightmares—than the fleeting pleasure of numbness, you'd drop it like you would a handful of hot coals. But illusions tip the scale in the other direction, painting a rose-tinted picture that the momentary alcohol is worth the aftermath.

I mention illusions so frequently because they're genuinely the heart of it. We can't simply label ourselves "weak-willed." If that were the problem, we'd expect discipline to fix it. But so many strong, successful individuals remain stuck in heavy drinking or dangerous binge cycles. They can have ironclad willpower in other areas—like forging a career, raising a family, or mastering a sport—yet they can't seem to break free from their nightcap. That's because the beliefs around alcohol run deeper than a conscious vow. They're tied to primal urges, comforting rituals, and social acceptance.

Once you accept that illusions must be dismantled rather than suppressed, you might approach this entire journey differently. If you still see booze as a "treat," giving it up can feel like your life is being robbed of flavor. Instead, you want to see it for what it truly is—a slow-acting toxin that manipulates your brain's reward circuitry, dulls your capacity to deal with reality, and ironically expands the problems it pretends to fix. With each passing day, you become more aware that the taste is nothing special (you have to hide it with sugar or fruit juice), the alcohol isn't genuine relaxation, and the purported social benefits often lead to regretful texts, lost wallets, or drunken arguments.

Shifting to that perspective is rarely an overnight epiphany, though threshold moments can jolt you into taking the first step. Real, lasting transformation typically unfolds as you keep noticing how illusions operate. Maybe you start paying closer attention to your thoughts right before you pour a drink, noticing the rationalizations you produce. Or you observe the grating taste that your sweet mixer tries to disguise. Over time, you might wake up one morning realizing that the lies have lost a chunk of their power. The desire to drink just isn't there. You no longer need to constantly push it away with raw willpower.

It's reminiscent of a child who was once terrified to sleep without a night-light. The fear vanished once they learned there was nothing lurking in the dark. Fear is replaced by calm knowledge. So it can be with the illusions of alcohol. Where you once dreaded a life without the crutch, you can come to see that the crutch was making your limp worse, not better. From there, you might find that other aspects of your life shift as well. With that daily alcohol gone, you have more energy, more creative juices, or simply more time to do things you've been putting off. Some folks dive into new hobbies, reclaim their passion for reading, start a small business, or invest in deeper relationships. Freed from the mental fog, they realize they've been functioning at half capacity for years.

Now, let's circle back to the role your own threshold moments played in bringing you to this text. You might have had a brush with medical anxiety, or a child's revelation in the form of a picture, or an exasperated spouse who threatened to leave if you don't get it together. Whatever it was, it created enough "pain" to outmatch the illusions for a short time. And here you are, exploring the possibility of a sober life. That's a big step, but as I experienced personally, fear and acute pain can fade. If you rely solely on them to carry you, you might relapse the moment normalcy returns. Instead, see them as catalysts to start questioning your illusions.

Alcohol is cunning and glacially patient. It creeps up slowly, letting you rationalize each new level of dependence. You rarely notice you've gone from not drinking on weekdays to one glass a night, then a bottle, and eventually a multi-bottle habit. The beliefs whisper, "You're in control, this is normal, you deserve it." By the time you sense the depth of your predicament, it can feel overwhelming. But delusions, once unmasked, lose their ability to seduce. That's the quiet revolution you might be about to undertake.

Maybe in a few weeks or months, you'll reach a point where the tang of booze on someone else's breath is a mild turn-off rather than a tempting aroma. The smell might remind you of a hazy time when you believed you needed that crutch, stirring a faint sympathy for those still trapped. Or maybe you'll recall the "wine connoisseur" identity you once embraced and chuckle at how seriously you took the swirl-and-sniff routine, convincing yourself you discerned mystical flavors of oak and fruit, when mostly you were burying the bitterness of ethanol under romantic illusions. You might shake your head at the memory of how you used to mix whiskey into your theater soda so that no moment of your day was free of alcohol.

This does not mean you must become a zealot, preaching the evils of alcohol to everyone at every gathering. People might not be ready to hear it, and some might lash out if you challenge their lies. The real peace you find is internal, an unshakeable knowledge that you're done playing that losing game. If someone at a party says, "Oh, come on, just one drink," you can politely say no without feeling you're giving anything up. That's the difference between wanting to not want it and actually not wanting it. The second is liberation; the first is a torturous limbo.

So as you continue reading and reflecting, keep an eye out for the illusions you once accepted at face value. Let them crack. Notice the empty taste alcohol leaves behind, the dryness hidden by sugar, the so-called relaxation that often ends in dehydration and restless sleep, the illusions about increased confidence that lead to embarrassing karaoke or ill-advised text messages. The more illusions you expose, the less you'll rely on threshold moments to scare you straight. You'll settle into a stable understanding: alcohol never gave you anything that your own mind and spirit couldn't provide more reliably, without the toxic aftermath.

Over time, you'll find the greatest feeling is not the fleeting sense of euphoria in the first drink, but the enduring sense of control when you recognize, "I don't need that in my life at all." That's the moment the balance of pain and pleasure flips forever in your favor.

Chapter 10: Deconstructing the Addiction

It's fascinating how alcohol has become woven into the fabric of modern life, camouflaged as a harmless accessory for relaxation and social fun. We learn from an early age that grown-ups celebrate promotions, birthdays, and even the end of a rough day with a glass or two of something boozy. If you step back, though, it's a bit perplexing: we're talking about a mind-altering, addictive depressant that many of us consume daily without a second thought. That might strike you as perfectly ordinary until you start questioning the illusions that keep this ritual afloat. How did we reach a point where ingesting a toxic chemical each evening seems more normal than not doing so?

The architecture of this deception relies on a few pillars. One critical piece is the collective conditioning that starts long before we're legally old enough to drink. Even if your parents didn't teach you explicitly that wine or beer are must-haves for every meal, you were still bombarded with subtle messages from television shows, adverts, and the people you grew up around. Maybe you witnessed them pouring a glass whenever they got home, cracking open a cold one after mowing the lawn, or telling you that "it's not a real party without champagne." Young minds absorb these cues like sponges. By the time you have your first sip, you've already formed a bedrock belief that "everyone drinks," and thus it can't be that harmful.

It's not only the environment in the home; entire industries pump vast resources into ensuring we keep swallowing the narrative. Alcohol marketing is a multi-billion-dollar juggernaut. Companies employ bright, energetic commercials featuring attractive, confident people who appear to be living life at full tilt—singing in nightclubs, dancing on beaches, flirting as the sun sets behind them. If you look closely, the adverts rarely state anything specific about the product's taste. They show you a picture of a perfect lifestyle and quietly associate it with the bottle. Our lizard brain, the part that loves social acceptance and physical pleasure, thinks, "That could be me if I pick up that brand." The commercial ends, our rational mind tries to dismiss it as just marketing fluff, but the subconscious has already stored the seductive image. Next time we walk by a bar, or see that brand in a supermarket, a small voice in our head recalls that bright scene and whispers that we, too, could capture some of that stardust.

Another dimension that helps alcohol trick us is the glorification of moderate daily drinking. There's this deep-rooted myth that a small dose of wine or beer each day is not just safe but potentially beneficial. Media headlines tout new "studies" every few months suggesting that a glass of red wine might help you live longer or reduce stress. This sliver of data gets blown out of proportion by laypeople and marketing teams alike. Meanwhile, the bigger story—how even moderate alcohol intake is linked to a wide range of health risks—goes mostly unnoticed. If you challenge someone about their nightly glass, they might wave you off with a casual statement about red wine having antioxidants. But step back for a second: nobody is out there touting daily low-dose arsenic to boost your immune system, yet we regularly parrot these questionable half-truths that paint a depressant as a health tonic.

The social dimension, too, is potent. We are pack animals, shaped by the beliefs and behaviors of those we care about and spend time with. If all your colleagues gather after work to decompress with pints or cocktails, you can feel compelled to blend in, not wanting to be the odd one out with a soda in hand. If your family events revolve around large bottles of wine poured from the start of the evening until bedtime, it's easy to see that as your normal. Repeated scenarios like that make it tricky to step away and ask if you'd be happier without alcohol. Everyone else is raising a glass, so why not me?

Part of the con also rests on alcohol's short-term effect of dulling stress or anxiety. We have an illusory sense that it "relaxes" us, while in truth, it's more like the alcohol combined with an eventual rebound effect of increased anxiety once it wears off causes us to feel more stress not less. Because we're latching onto that initial warm, fuzzy alcohol, we believe we're achieving calm. Then, 24 hours later, as mild withdrawal sets in, we interpret those jitters as "stress." Another glass seems to fix the tension, creating a loop in which alcohol is used to repair the agitation that alcohol itself caused. This cyclical nature is the lifeblood of daily drinking: we think we're solving daily stresses, when actually we're perpetuating them.

We also have to factor in how normal it's become to use alcohol in every facet of modern life. If you look at ancient rituals, they might have used small amounts of alcohol for special ceremonies. Now we use it for nearly every occasion, big or small. A coworker's birthday? Someone inevitably suggests a happy hour. A random Sunday brunch with friends? The table is incomplete without mimosas. That casual reliance means we almost never see how bizarre it is. If someone proposed mixing a mild sedative into our cereal each morning, we'd recoil in horror. Yet we think nothing of swirling a shot of potent ethanol in a pretty glass each night.

We also can't ignore the role of beliefs around "deservedness." People say, "I deserve a drink," especially if they've had a tough day or accomplished a challenging task. Alcohol, in that sense, becomes a reward, a treat at the end of a punishing shift or a chaotic day with the kids. The bizarre part is that many of us can't articulate why alcohol is a real treat. We rarely say we "deserve" a comedown or we "deserve" a mild poisoning. But because it's hammered into us that relaxing = sipping a drug, we embrace the logic without question.

Moreover, fear of being labeled or singled out fosters the delusions. We cling to illusions like "I'm not that bad," or "I only drink socially," or "At least I don't drink in the morning." Because the alternative is a dreaded identity as "someone with a drinking problem." Nobody wants that label. Alcohol, ironically, provides a way to block out this creeping doubt. So a perfect loop forms: the lies feed continued consumption, which helps us forget or rationalize any alarm bells, which further cements our illusions. Days become weeks, and suddenly months become years of daily alcohol.

Another cunning trick is that alcohol, while dangerous, rarely kills overnight. If we took a shot of something that caused immediate convulsions, society would quickly figure out that it's harmful. But alcohol often kills slowly, chipping away at the liver, the cardiovascular system, mental health, or relationships. We blame everything but the sedative: we blame stress at the office, the kids' demands, the cost of living. Meanwhile, day after day, we swirl that glass, feeling we have no other path to unwind. Because we're not seeing immediate, catastrophic results, we hold the illusions intact. They only sometimes shatter if a dramatic event occurs—like a health scare or a drunk-driving incident. Yet even then, the illusions can be so tenacious that some still find ways to justify continued use.

Throughout this, the marketing machine continues to hum, the social norms continue to feed it, and the alcohol continues to lull us into believing that everything's fine. It's not a single factor. Rather, it's a tapestry of cultural cues, biological cravings, emotional reliance, and non-stop messages from every direction telling us how "normal" it is to ingest an addictive depressant on a daily basis. Over time, we barely pause to notice how illogical it is. Only when we strip away each piece—seeing that it's not actually relaxing, that it's not always so tasty, that we don't need alcohol to celebrate or cope—do the beliefs crumble. That's the moment the con unravels. It becomes obvious we've been collectively hoodwinked into believing something bizarre and harmful is not just acceptable but practically essential.

In the interest of honesty, I will forewarn you of my intention to use a sneaky persuasion technique on you called a 'presupposition.' Salesmen use these types of questions to appear to be offering you a choice when, in fact, all the responses serve the same purpose. A good example of a presupposition that might have been used on you, perhaps unwittingly, as a young child by your parents would be, 'Do you want to go to bed now or in ten minutes' time?' The question appears to give you the luxury of a choice, but all outcomes result in the same thing — you in bed within ten minutes.

My sneaky question to you is: do you want to stop drinking completely or just cut down a bit and repeat this process every time you lose control again until you stop? Obviously, I am trying to gently push you in the direction I know you should go, and despite telling you the option to cut down has repeated failure built into it, your ego still thinks it is in control and can handle anything. Be certain of this: your ego doesn't want you to stop drinking because it predicts that will result in pain/fear in the future.

I know many readers would prefer to cut down rather than stop, but the only logical solution is for you to step out of the mousetrap and never get back in. If you are dependent on alcohol and you don't want to stop, you have not quite grasped the problem. If a heroin addict came up to you and said, 'I have decided to only use drugs on a Tuesday and never any other day,' how confident are you that if you bumped into them again in a year's time that would be still the case? Alcoholism is a binary condition; it is either on or off. You can't be a little bit alcoholic in the same way you can't be a little bit pregnant!

You may need to read this book over and over before you get to this point and your decision is in harmony with my advice. Quitting completely really is the best option for you, but you must come to that decision on your own. You can't be convinced by me, your family, or friends, and nobody can order you to take this stance. It has to come deep from within you. If you currently feel that you are still at the point where you believe you can control the situation, or that you enjoy it too much to stop completely, don't panic or beat yourself up too much. You are not alone in this struggle. In my online community, you will find people who are in the same position as you. Nobody has ever developed a drinking problem and then woken up the next morning and cured it in a eureka moment of perfection.

Part of the journey to sobriety is experiencing the futility of trying to find a way to keep the bits you like while removing the consequences you don't want. It is like trying to bail out the Titanic with a bucket; for a while, you may believe you are making headway, but very soon you start to see that you can't possibly succeed. I tried dozens and dozens of different buckets before I realized that the good parts of drinking go hand in hand with the bad, and you can't have one without the other.

Here are just a few of the buckets I thought might bail out my sinking ship:

- I will only drink on the weekends.
- I will only drink socially and never at home.
- I will drink a glass of water for every glass of alcohol I drink.
- I will take three months off the drink each year.
- I will only drink beer and no wine or spirits.
- I will only drink wine and only with food as part of a meal.

Add to that list of ridiculous theories the expensive prescription drugs I turned to. The first I tried was Disulfiram, which interferes with the way your liver processes alcohol and makes you violently ill if you drink. The problem with this drug is that it relies on your discipline to take it every morning. Alcoholics are not known for their discipline). Initially, if I knew there was a big party or social occasion I was going to, I just wouldn't take it (and so begins the failure routine. Predictably, I then loosened my rules further by only taking it Monday to Friday, allowing myself to drink at the weekends. I convinced myself that I deserved a treat at the weekends for being so good during the week.

The next stage of my defiance came when I resented the drug for preventing me from drinking during the week. I experimented with it and found that I could just about tolerate a small beer while taking it. Any more than that and the side effects would knock me flat on my back. One night I pushed it a little further and had a large beer and a glass of wine. Within 20 minutes, my head was pounding, my face blushing bright red, while my heart felt like it was trying to beat its way out of my chest cavity. For a moment, I honestly thought I might die, and the only solution was to lie in a dark room motionless for several hours until the effects subsided.

I tried other drugs, such as acamprosate calcium, which interferes with the release of dopamine, essentially taking all the pleasure out of drinking. Over time it renders your favorite tipple as pleasurable as a soft drink, and logically you only want to drink one of those when you are thirsty. Again, with this drug, the willpower or discipline required to take a daily tablet that ruins the very thing you are addicted to is a significant challenge. Add to that some pretty horrendous side effects such as dizzy spells, insomnia, dry mouth, and worse, and you start to think that feeling this bad to stay off the drink is simply not worth it.

Whether it's crazy routines or pills, these methods are all simply evidence of the ego's delusion that it is in some way in control. All these methods use some form of willpower that can't possibly work because, underneath the smokescreen, you still believe that you are being deprived of what you believe to be the benefits of alcohol.

Remember, there is no such thing as failure. Things that go wrong are just events in the past, a period we are no longer concerned with. If you finish reading this book and go three weeks without a drink and then slip up, the natural temptation (and the ego's opinion) is to think that the solutions in this book don't work, you are not strong enough, or you are always destined to be a problem drinker. Recognize this belief for what it is: the conscious mind trying to predict the future — a skill it simply doesn't have. If you fall off the wagon – big deal. Dust yourself down and carry on. When you wake in the morning, what is the point of beating yourself up about that mistake you made the night before? The past no longer exists.

Presumably, you haven't woken up with a bottle in your hand having been drinking in your sleep somehow, so right there in that moment (where all of life is lived), you are not a drinker. Equally, now that we know that the future also doesn't exist and will never exist, the fact that you had a drink the night before has no bearing on whether you will have one later that day, tomorrow, the next day, or ever again. Take each moment as it comes; every second that you decide you don't want to drink is a success.

The secret to stopping drinking is the same as the secret to getting anything else in life that you want, and this is to remain in the moment. Don't make predictions about what sort of person you will be in the future. I wouldn't ask you to predict what will happen tomorrow any more than I would ask you to perform open-heart surgery on me; you simply don't have the skills to help me. (Of course, I am recklessly playing the numbers here. One day, this book will land with an eminent heart surgeon, and he will be mortally offended by that statement.) Your journey out of the mousetrap happens by being aware of your egoic mind. Every time you find your mind wandering into the future or past, observe this happening from the point of view of an outsider. Disconnect yourself from the process; catch your ego at work.

For your conscious mind to have any power at all, it needs you to believe that you and it are the same thing. If you see it for what it is, a minor part of your mind at work, then it loses all its influence over you. Every time you catch your mind starting to worry, predict, or reflect on past events and deliberately pull yourself back into the present moment, you reduce its power over you by a fraction of one percent.

For most people, the conscious mind seizes control of them tens of thousands of times a day, and so this process isn't a magic bullet cure. I can't promise if you do this ten times, 20 times, or 50 times, you will be cured, but then you didn't become alcohol dependent overnight, and no system out there can hope to restore the correct balance in a similarly brief time period. Most other detox systems require a period of withdrawal, often called going 'cold turkey,' which for an alcoholic is at best torturous, and in worst-case scenarios can be fatal.

My method starts with your deep-seated desire to end this painful cycle and slowly deconstructs the obstacles which are preventing you from achieving your goal. Slowly, over time, as you keep resisting the attempted hijackings by your egoic mind, you will feel a sense of peace begin to build. Once you get beyond the physical dependence on alcohol, your urge to drink is generated by the wants and needs of the ego. As this diminishes, so does your desire for alcohol.

A popular question at this point is: 'How long will it take?' I can't predict the future any more than you can, so I won't even try. For most people, once they understand that everything they previously believed about alcohol having a benefit was a big fat lie and can see that a chemical imbalance is causing pain for their ego to respond to – they simply stop. For a great many people, that happens directly after reading this book. Others need a few weeks for the information to sink in, and others read the book several times before the penny drops.

Whether it takes a day or a year is irrelevant; you will find this simple process will not only remove your damaging patterns around alcohol but also all other negative habits too. Denying the ego will slowly repair everything from relationships to finances. If you would like to delve into greater detail about how it works, I suggest reading my books: Swallow the Happy Pill and the Light Beyond.

Once your conscious mind begins to loosen its grip on your perception of reality, this system becomes easier and easier. The secret to success is to stick at this long enough to become aware of a shift in power.

Chapter 11: Balance, Not Battle

One warm evening, I found myself standing by a quiet river, watching how the water flowed around a large boulder in its path. The current didn't try to smash the rock out of the way; it simply met the obstacle with gentle persistence, sliding around it and continuing on. There was no struggle in the water's movement, yet over time that solid stone would wear down from the constant, patient flow. In that moment, I realised I was witnessing a lesson from the Tao Te Ching in real time – a lesson I desperately needed in my journey to stop drinking. I had been fighting my problem drinking like a man at war, all willpower and resistance, when perhaps I needed to be more like that water: patient, adaptable, and quietly unstoppable.

For years I approached quitting alcohol as a battle to be fought. Every morning I'd wake up vowing to defeat the "enemy" (the bottle) by brute force. By evening, I'd lost another battle, drained from the day's stresses and marching back to the fridge as if in a trance. It felt like two parts of me were arm-wrestling nonstop – the part that knew I needed to quit versus the part that insisted I needed a drink to relax or cope. This exhausting stalemate persisted for an interminable period. The ancient Taoist sages, however, would probably chuckle at my approach. Lao Tzu, the author of the Tao Te Ching, teaches that many of life's struggles are best resolved not by aggressive force but by humble surrender. "The hard and stubborn is the disciple of death, while the soft and yielding is the disciple of life," he wrote. In other words, rigidity and fighting can break you, but yielding – letting go of the rope in a tug-of-war – can actually secure your survival and victory. At first, the idea of surrendering to win felt like a contradiction. My ego screamed that surrender was the same as giving up. But what if "giving up" the fight meant peace instead of defeat? I started to see that my white-knuckle willpower method was a form of stiffness. I was so rigidly focused on resisting alcohol that I would snap under pressure, much like a dry branch that refuses to bend in a storm. The Tao Te Ching often uses water as a metaphor for wisdom: "Nothing in the world is as soft and accommodating as water, and yet for overcoming the hard and inflexible, there is nothing more effective... the yielding wears away at the unyielding". What a revelation – maybe I didn't have to meet alcohol head-on with gritted teeth. Instead, I could try absorbing and flowing around the urge, the way water finds a path around rock. I decided to experiment with this approach the next time a craving hit. Rather than tensely repeating "Don't drink, don't drink" like a mantra, I acknowledged the urge when it came. "Ah, there you are," I found myself saying to the craving, almost as if greeting an old, bothersome friend. Instead of immediately wrestling with it, I allowed it to just be, like a cloud passing through the sky of my mind. I remembered a core Taoist idea: when you stop resisting, you stop fueling the thing you're resisting. By not pouring my energy into a battle with the craving, I robbed that craving of its power. Sure enough, it passed on its own, much sooner and with less drama than when I would fight it. This was my first taste of what Lao Tzu might call "effortless action" – doing by not over-doing, conquering by yielding.

A big reason we struggle in quitting drinking is our old nemesis, the ego. Our ego hates to lose. It hates to feel weak or out of control. Ironically, drinking often began as a misguided attempt by the ego to assert control – to control our mood, our stress, our social image. (How many times did I drink just to fit in or to seem funnier and more confident?) Over time, that illusion of control flips. The drink that we thought we controlled ends up controlling us. Admitting this feels like an ego defeat: "How could I, a successful adult, be unable to handle something as common as beer?" The ego flares up at such a thought, and pride can keep us from acknowledging the problem or accepting help. Ancient wisdom advises us to tame the ego with humility and self-honesty. The Stoic philosopher Epictetus bluntly told his students, "Sober up. You're a slave!" – slave to whatever masters your impulses. It's a jarring statement, but he was right. When alcohol held the leash, I wasn't making free choices; my cravings were.

Seneca, another Stoic, wrote that "Freedom is the prize we are working for: not being a slave to anything — not to compulsion, not to chance events". In other words, true freedom means no external substance or random urge is calling the shots. If my hand was reaching for whiskey against my own better judgment, how free was I, really? Lao Tzu would agree on the importance of self-mastery. "He who conquers others is strong; he who conquers himself is mighty," he reminds us. To conquer myself, I had to outwit the ego and its lies. And oh, the lies it would spin to justify a drink! "I've had a rough day, I deserve a reward." "Just one won't hurt." "You can quit tomorrow; tonight, let's celebrate." Sound familiar? These are the ego's classic bargaining tactics. The word "believe" even has a "lie" right in the middle. The beliefs I held about alcohol ("I need it to relax," "I can't enjoy a party without it") were just that – beliefs, not facts. They were conditioned stories, repeated until they felt like truth. Once I learned to question them, many turned out to be outright lies or half-truths my mind clung to. One by one, I started dismantling these beliefs with simple reality checks. Did alcohol truly relax me? Perhaps for twenty minutes I'd feel a false glow – but a few hours later I'd be awake at 3 AM, heart racing and anxiety through the roof as the withdrawal kicked in. Some "relaxation." Did I really become more fun and witty after a few drinks, or did I just think I did? (There's nothing quite like recalling a tipsy joke you told, and realising it wasn't that funny – maybe even the opposite.) With each honest observation, the myth of alcohol's benefits cracked a little more. I began to see booze not as a friend or a prize, but as bait on a hook. What it promised in the moment (stress relief, confidence) was just a lure. The real payoff was hangovers, regret, and a growing emptiness. As the illusion lifted, my desire to drink started to lift as well. After all, who actively craves being duped? This is where self-awareness blossomed into a powerful tool, just as the Tao and the Stoics alike insist. "He who knows himself is wise," Lao Tzu wrote, and I finally understood that knowing myself included knowing my triggers and my patterns without judgment. I noticed I tended to reach for a drink when I felt bored or unappreciated. Boredom, for me, was actually a disguise for a lack of purpose, and feeling unappreciated was a trigger for my ego to throw a pity party. These were things I could address without alcohol. By picking up a neglected hobby or calling a friend, I could deal with boredom in a healthy way. By reminding myself of the gratitude I have for the people who do care about me, I could deflate that ego balloon of self-pity. Each time I did this, I was practicing conquering myself – gently, not with brute force, but with understanding and self-compassion.

One of the beautiful teachings of the Tao Te Ching is to observe nature and learn from it. In nature, everything has a rhythm: day and night, seasons of growth and rest. There's a balance at play that doesn't require micromanagement. No tree forces itself to grow; it just absorbs sunlight and water, and growth happens. No lion feels guilty for resting all day after a big meal; it lives in tune with its needs. When I was drinking, I had fallen out of tune with my own natural rhythm. I'd artificially push my moods up with alcohol's initial buzz, then crash down into gloomy lethargy as it wore off. My sleep cycle was a mess, energy levels all over the place. I was like a plant being yanked up and down instead of allowed to grow steadily. Reconnecting with a natural rhythm became a cornerstone of my happy sober life. I started honoring the balance my body and mind needed. That meant regular sleep, decent nutrition, and yes, sometimes just sitting with my feelings instead of trying to chemically escape them. Taoist wisdom often speaks of returning to the simple and the fundamental. "Manifest plainness, embrace simplicity… have few desires," Lao Tzu advises. In modern terms, I took this as guidance to simplify my life and be content with less drama and stimulation. Instead of chasing every party or drowning every irritation in drink, I learned to be okay with a quiet evening, a cup of tea, and my own thoughts for company. It wasn't boring – it was peaceful. What I had once labelled as "dull" I now recognised as serenity. This shift did something miraculous: it removed a lot of the temptation to drink in the first place. The Stoics have a saying akin to Taoist thought: "Freedom is not procured by the full enjoyment of what is desired, but by controlling desire." In other words, you don't become free by giving your cravings everything they want – you become free by wanting less. When my life became fuller with genuine activities and rest, I naturally wanted alcohol less. It wasn't some white-knuckled act of constant denial anymore; I simply found more rewarding things to do and healthier ways to handle stress. The desire shrank on its own, which made staying sober dramatically easier. It's like I stopped feeding a stray dog at my door – eventually, it stopped coming around as often. I also learned the value of patience from nature and Taoism. Just as seasons change gradually, I didn't transform from problem drinker to sage overnight. There were days I felt like nothing was improving, that I was still the same anxious mess – just minus the booze. But beneath the surface, like seeds in winter soil, the changes were taking root. Each sober sunrise was a little victory, even if it felt ordinary. Over weeks and months, these small victories – clearer mornings, a genuine laugh with a friend I remembered fully, a quiet sense of pride at saying "no thanks, I'll have a soda" – accumulated into real momentum. The Tao Te Ching teaches that even a great journey begins with a single step, and I was finally taking those steps consistently. Tiny, unglamorous steps, but each one carried me further from the misery and imbalance that drinking had brought, and closer to the balanced life I wanted.

There's a wonderful paradox at play here. Initially, I thought sobriety was all about discipline – almost a militaristic self-control. And discipline does have a role, but not in the harsh way I imagined. Instead of a discipline of punishment, I found a discipline of understanding. When you truly understand what alcohol does to you and why you turned to it, the resolve to not drink comes naturally, almost effortlessly. I said in my first book 'Alcohol Lied To Me', "The very idea of willpower is an oxymoron. There is actually no power at all in willpower."

I was pointing out that white-knuckle willpower alone is a weak strategy; it often fails because it's just you fighting yourself. Real power comes from changing your perspective – from knowledge and mindset, not muscle. I found this to be absolutely true. When my mind truly shifted to see alcohol for what it is (a liar and a thief of happiness) and to see sobriety for what it could be (a genuine, lasting contentment), staying sober no longer felt like a chore. It became my natural state, and drinking started to seem like the unnatural, bizarre thing. To maintain this healthier mindset, I borrowed practices from both Stoicism and Taoism. From the Stoics, I embraced the habit of morning reflections and evening reviews. Each morning I might remind myself, "No matter what happens today, it's up to me how I respond. A bad day is not an excuse to drink; it's a reason to apply wisdom." Each evening I would calmly note how the day went – did I stay true to myself? Did I encounter any temptation, and how did I handle it? No judgment, just observation, much like a sage observing the shifting of clouds. From Taoism, I embraced the idea of wu wei, or effortless action. I started trusting myself more – trusting that I didn't have to obsess every hour about staying sober. I set my intention to live free of alcohol and then went about my day, flowing through tasks, staying present. If a tough situation arose (say, a tense work meeting or an invite to a boozy dinner), I didn't panic. I reminded myself I could stay aligned with the natural choice I'd made. In a sense, I let go of overthinking it. Paradoxically, by not obsessing on sobriety every second, I felt more at ease being sober. It became normal life, not a special project. Dry humour helped a lot too. Whenever I caught the inner voice romanticising a drink – "Wouldn't a cold beer be nice right now?" – I learned to answer with a bit of wit to disarm it. "Ah yes, beer, that well-known solution to all life's problems," I'd think sarcastically, rolling my eyes at myself. Or I'd visualise a cartoonish evil clown – like a twisted inner jester – offering me a poison chalice while honking a horn. It sounds ridiculous, but that was the point. By laughing at the absurdity of what my addiction was urging me to do ("Here, have some poison, it'll help!"), the temptation lost a lot of its grip. Humor turned out to be a pressure valve, releasing the tension. It's hard to fall for a trick once you've had a good laugh at it.

Integrating the Taoist and Stoic wisdom into my recovery wasn't a one-time event; it became a way of life. Each day I strive to live in balance: not too tense, not too lax. I respect that I'm human – I will experience highs and lows, and I don't need to blot either out with alcohol. If a feeling is uncomfortable, I recall Lao Tzu's teaching to "leave the world alone" – in essence, to stop fussing and let things be. Emotions, like the weather, pass on their own if you let them. If a celebratory mood comes, I embrace it fully without the thought that it could be made "better" by a drink. It's already good as it is, in fact far better when I'm fully present. I also keep in mind the Stoic notion that external things (like a social event or a piece of bad news) don't dictate my reaction – I do. I can't control the external world or other people's drinking, but I can control where I steer my own ship. A storm might come, but I can choose to furl the sails, batten the hatches, and ride it out rather than drunkenly leap overboard. This sense of control over my choices is deeply empowering, and it grows each day I exercise it. In the end, the ancient philosophies converged on a simple truth: overcoming problem drinking wasn't about being superhuman or waging an endless war with myself. It was about understanding the nature of the struggle, and then transcending it. I learned to step aside and let my true self – the part of me that sincerely wants health, peace, and freedom – take the lead. Lao Tzu's gentle voice, reminding me to be like water and find the path of least resistance, and Marcus Aurelius or Epictetus reminding me to master my mind and desires, became like a wise council I could consult anytime in my thoughts. If you had told me years ago that a 2,500-year-old Chinese text and the musings of Roman philosophers could help me quit drinking, I might have laughed (and likely raised a glass in jest). But here I stand, genuinely laughing – not in disbelief, but in joy. Joy at the surprising journey that brought me to a sober life that feels natural and fulfilling. Joy at the balance I've found between effort and ease, discipline and surrender. And perhaps most of all, joy at the quiet mind that I wake up with each day, no longer at war with itself. In your own path to a happy sober life, I invite you to consider this blend of ancient wisdom. Take what resonates: maybe the flowing water imagery helps you in a tough moment, or a Stoic mantra steels your resolve on a tricky Friday night. Use whatever works. These teachings have lasted millennia for a reason – they speak to something fundamentally human in us. And overcoming an addiction, at its heart, is a deeply human triumph. It's a return to our natural state of balance, a homecoming to ourselves. So, when the road gets rough, remember the Taoist sage's gentle guidance and the Stoic's stern wisdom. Balance, not battle. Flow, don't force. Surrender, and win. With a little dry humour and a lot of self-honesty, you might find that the obstacles which once loomed so large have gradually been worn down to pebbles under your steady, patient current. And on the other side of that once-troubled water lies the happy, sober life you knew was waiting for you all along.

Chapter 12: Expensive Poison

I remember the day I finally mustered the courage to calculate just how much I'd been spending on alcohol. For the longest time, I avoided sitting down with a pen and paper to face that brutal figure. It felt safer not to see what I was pouring into a habit I had convinced myself was a benign indulgence. That convenient ignorance is typical: when we're still in the thrall of drinking, we shy away from anything that might expose the truth – especially the ugly math that shows how much money is getting swallowed by a daily ritual of poison.

Western culture tends to prop up this fantasy that alcohol is a harmless pleasure meant for social gatherings. The reality is more sinister. It can become such a powerful sedative that, if you're not careful, you can't even bring yourself to the doctor, knowing full well you might be told to quit. You'd rather risk your health than endure the slightest suggestion that alcohol might not be your friend. That's how sly this drug can be: it keeps us in denial, feeding us pleasant illusions while stealthily causing havoc in our bodies, relationships, and bank accounts.

At my worst point, I was consuming two bottles of wine every night, plus a weekend bonus of a bottle of whiskey for good measure. When I finally did the sums, it turned out I was spending roughly twenty-three dollars a day on alcohol. That's one hundred sixty-one dollars a week, seven hundred twenty-four dollars a month, basically nine thousand dollars a year. Even now, it stuns me to think about it. But here's the thing that really freaked me out: learning I was throwing that kind of money at my habit wouldn't have stopped me from drinking. That's possibly the most frightening part. I might have been depressed about the number, but I would have carried on.

If I'd kept going, I probably would have topped up that daily consumption further, chasing the buzz that was diminishing as my tolerance grew. It's not a stretch to say I could have spent over eighty thousand dollars across a decade, all to feed the same nightly routine. Even that estimate is rosy, ignoring the random splurges on fancy bottles I bought whenever I found an excuse to treat myself – birthdays, anniversaries, or just because it was Friday. And it's not only the money lost on alcohol itself. There are the "missed opportunities," too: special trips I never took, family luxuries I said I couldn't afford, or the restless nights that robbed me of real rest so I performed at half my capacity the next day.

The scariest part is how the cost didn't even deter me. Had I stumbled upon my own spreadsheet of self-destruction, it would have crushed my mood but changed nothing. Because when you're heavily invested in this drug, harsh facts rarely penetrate. You buy into any excuses to keep the wine flowing. The lies run so deep that you'll ignore the daily drain on your finances, your relationships, your health – all for that fleeting sedative effect. I used to moan about how we couldn't afford better family vacations, ignoring that I was quite literally drinking our holiday fund every day.

It's not always about the money. If that were the only drawback to drinking, you'd just weigh it up and decide if you'd rather have a fatter wallet or a glass of Bordeaux. Alcohol's real devastation is bigger. In my case, the immediate consequence was how it turned me into a zombie by eight or nine in the evening. I'd open the first bottle of wine at 6:00 pm and be dozing off not long after finishing the second. If you think about it, that's more than a hundred extra hours a month stolen from my life. Over the course of ten years, I estimate I lost over nine thousand hours – entire months of potential experiences, wiped away as I collapsed face-down on my pillow in an intoxicated slump.

It's a sobering notion, if you'll excuse the pun. Once you start quantifying the hours you spent unconscious or half-present with your family, you begin to see that alcohol's cost isn't limited to your bank statements. If you're a parent, the thought of forfeiting precious time with your kids is devastating. Those memories I missed out on, the bedtime stories never read, the silly nighttime jokes we might have shared – I traded them all for a glass or two (or more). People like to call alcohol a "social drug," but that's the paradox: it lulled me away from being social with the people I valued most.

Let's ramp that up to a more painful illustration. If you're a mother or father, imagine the horror of losing your child tomorrow and never seeing them again. It sounds brutal, but I want you to feel that pang because it underscores how invaluable time with our loved ones truly is. Now, if months later, a strange miracle allowed you to buy a single hour with your child, what would you pay? Would there be any number too high to secure that fleeting moment? If you're like me, you'd consider that hour priceless. But each day that you spend passed out or absent because of booze is an hour you'll never recover. I lost thousands of them with my kids. If you want to see me turn red with anger at myself, just bring up how many days, nights, and weekends I basically forfeited to a wine bottle.

That's my story, but your poison might function differently. Maybe alcohol turns you restless at night, or maybe you become moody and lash out at people you care about. Regardless, the trade is the same: you're giving up something precious in exchange for a short-lived effect that leaves you tired, broke, or regretful the next morning. Over time, it piles up into a mountain of regret. And for what? A fleeting sense of numbness at the end of a stressful day?

I recall, to this day, the anger that washed over me when I finally recognized how thoroughly I'd been cheated. Some days, it was enough to make me slam my fist on the table. A harmless glass of wine, that cultural staple, had effectively robbed me of both money and time with the people I loved. It was a betrayal I had willingly participated in. It's not that I want to wallow in guilt, but if you're currently buying into the delusions, I hope you see how high the stakes are.

Let's shift gears and focus on you: what has alcohol stolen from you so far? Is it your peace of mind, your sense of humor, your marriage, your friendships, or that job you might have aced if you weren't nursing hangovers half the week? The list can get grim. But recognizing the theft is vital. Because for as long as we keep dressing alcohol up as a "little indulgence," we excuse its presence while it sinks its claws deeper into our finances, our relationships, and our mental health.

A friend once told me he was sure he spent no more than a few bucks a day on booze, so it couldn't be that big a deal. I suggested he tally all the hidden sips: the second beer he has with lunch, the glass of wine or two after dinner, the bigger sprees on the weekend. Suddenly, his daily average soared, and the monthly cost was no longer something to shrug at. Multiply it by a year, then consider if that money could have covered the credit card debt he's stressed about. Or paid for a family trip that might've created beautiful memories. Once you put it that way, it's hard to see your nightly glass in the same romantic light.

But the most harrowing part isn't the stolen money – it's the stolen opportunities. And each day we choose to keep ignoring the problem is another day lost. I call it "common drug addiction" because we've become so used to labeling it as a normal part of adult life. Yet it steals from us all the same. The bleak truth is, if you keep going on your current path, you might find yourself many years from now, aware of how many chances slipped through your fingers. That's not a comfortable epiphany.

Alcohol can also do a number on your sleeping patterns. In my case, I was physically drained all day because I'd pass out by eight or nine at night, toss and turn in a dehydrated haze, and struggle to get going the next morning. I used to daydream about finishing projects, or having quality time with my family, but it was virtually impossible when I'd given away my alert evening hours to a fog of alcohol. My life shrank to a repetitive cycle: come home from work, drink, pass out, drag myself to the office. It was a dull existence, and I only realized it once I stepped outside the bubble.

Now, let's circle back to that hardest question: If your child or someone dear to you were to vanish from your life tomorrow, how much would you pay for just one more hour with them? Most of us would tear open our wallets, liquidate savings, or do anything else. That's how invaluable genuine time is. Yet every night we dedicate to a bottle is effectively time we're forfeiting. It's gone forever. I look back and see thousands of hours poured away – hours I could have spent building memories with my kids. My chest tightens just thinking about it.

When the heartbreak of that truth finally landed on me, I needed a break. I felt cheated and furious. Alcohol had carried me along, whispering that it was harmless, necessary even. Meanwhile, it was siphoning away money, time, experiences, and the self-respect I might have nourished had I not been lost in that cycle.

Your own experience may differ, but I'll wager you can pinpoint at least one sphere of your life that has been compromised. Maybe it's your finances, maybe it's your health. Perhaps your spouse feels neglected, or your personal dreams have been postponed so many times you've forgotten what they were. If you wonder where all the funds or enthusiasm went, the culprit might be sitting in your refrigerator or perched on your kitchen counter. And it's cunning enough that you might not suspect the real extent of the theft unless you scrutinize it the way you're doing now.

At this juncture, people often get defensive. They'll claim, "But I only spend a few dollars a day on it. That's manageable." And maybe that's technically true. But think of it in the aggregate: a few dollars a day times 365 is easily over a grand a year, more if you're someone who tosses in an occasional $50 top-shelf purchase. Then there are the hidden extras: the drunken online shopping or food deliveries you regret in the morning, the cabs you hail when you're too buzzed to drive, the occasional bar tab that grows suspiciously high after just a few hours. Add it up, and it might exceed $3,000 a year. If I were to hand you $3,000 cash right now and say, "Do what you like with this," you'd have no shortage of ideas. A decent vacation, a chunk of debt cleared, a new laptop, an extra treat for the family. The difference is, you do already have that money – it's just being systematically funneled toward a beverage that, ironically, makes you less content in the long run.

So here's a challenge: do what I was too terrified to do when I was drinking heavily. Grab a piece of paper (or open a spreadsheet) and get brutally honest. Figure out your monthly or annual spend on alcohol. Don't cheat by ignoring your birthday bashes or festive blowouts. If you treat yourself to top-dollar liquor on those special occasions, factor that in. Tally the total. It might shock you. Now, imagine I gave you that exact amount in a bundle of cash. Would you funnel it back into booze, or would you send your kids to Disney World? Would you clear that pesky overdraft or invest it in something meaningful? That's your money, the fruits of your labor, quietly bleeding away night after night.

To make it more real, go online and find a picture that represents something you'd love to do with the recaptured cash. Maybe it's an image of a family holiday resort, or a dream home extension, or the front of your local college if you want to fund your kids' future. Print that image and stick it on your fridge or bathroom mirror. It's a tangible reminder that there's a direct trade-off between continuing to pay the "alcohol tax" each day and achieving that dream. If you ever tear that picture down without having lived that dream, ask yourself: which illusions did you allow back in?

It might be painful or embarrassing to realize how you've been misled, but pain can also be a catalyst. We only fight illusions when we finally see them for the shams they are.

Alcohol seduces us with talk of relaxation and sophistication. The truth is it's an expensive, cunning way to steal your nights, your weekends, your money, and your memories. The next time someone tries to frame it as a social essential, or a glorious treat, try to remember just how much it has already cost you or the people you care about. That memory might be all the motivation you need to walk away from the bottle and toward a life unburdened by that expensive, time-sucking alcohol.

In my case, the heartbreak of calculating all the money and days lost was enough to jolt me out of my sleep. I hated the feeling of looking at my children, imagining how many memories I'd sacrificed. But better to feel that sting now than to maintain beliefs for another decade. If you're on the fence, worrying about living a life without alcohol, consider that you're already giving it up anyway – you're giving up your finances, your health, or your precious hours with loved ones in exchange for a fleeting chemical kick. Do you want to keep paying that tab?

The road ahead may not be easy, but it's straightforward in principle. You face the truth of how this drug operates, and you decide you're done being robbed. That initial step might feel drastic because we're so deeply programmed to accept alcohol as normal, but the freedom on the other side is immense. Meanwhile, your wallet and your family will be quietly cheering.

Chapter 13: A Little External Help

Always remember, none of this is intended to replace professional medical care. Before making any big changes—especially if you have physical withdrawal symptoms such as tremors, severe sickness, or even hallucinations—seek help from a doctor. They can prescribe medication to reduce uncomfortable and potentially dangerous side effects while you go through withdrawal. That might sound like a slight inconvenience, but trust me, your safety comes first.

I'm assuming you picked up this book because you want a different relationship with alcohol—or perhaps to cut it out completely—but you're not entirely sure how to begin. By this point, I hope your inner resolve has strengthened. If you've read earlier sections, you're likely seeing alcohol for the insidious chemical it really is. You might even sense that you never want to touch that foul-tasting, life-sabotaging depressant again. Alternatively, you might still be holding out for that magical day when you can "drink responsibly" or cut down to a "safe level." Let me explain why such a plan has major pitfalls.

The first big thing to understand is "the kick." That's my shorthand for the withdrawal process—a period of discomfort following your last drink. Every addictive chemical has its own version of a kick. Some are short and intense; others can be drawn out and subtle. Heroin, for instance, is notorious for having a torturous withdrawal. Quitting heroin can feel like your entire body is being assaulted—imagine every nerve ending screaming at you—and you know you could end all that misery by just taking one more hit. That's why so many people remain trapped.

Alcohol's withdrawal, while still potentially serious, is generally milder when compared to hardcore street drugs. However, it's sneaky. People sometimes don't notice that the all-too-familiar "stress relief" they get from an after-work drink is mostly the alcohol that stops the daily withdrawal from the previous night's session. You might assume it's the typical ups and downs of daily life, but it's more accurate to see it as a miniature hangover that starts mid-afternoon. By the time you slide the key in your front door, you're halfway through the day's low, so you dash to the kitchen for that glass or two (or three), feeling instantly calmer. Of course you do—it's the chemical that's eliminating your withdrawal. This is the trap: once the first glass is gone, your body starts fresh withdrawal again, guaranteeing that you'll have to repeat the cycle tomorrow. Over time, that's how we get locked into daily usage.

Alcohol withdrawal has a peak period between roughly 24 and 48 hours after your last sip. The entire chemical imbalance can stretch on for up to two weeks, though it gradually diminishes after the initial few days. Usually, if you haven't had a drink for about two weeks, the physical part is mostly gone—close to zero, or so mild you might barely notice it. The trouble is, if you take "just one drink" at any point during that two-week window, you basically reset the clock, catapulting yourself back onto day one. That first glass yanks you right back into the loop. People who rely on sheer willpower typically miss this fact or dismiss it. They say, "I'll just have a small one tonight," not realizing they've triggered a fresh wave of withdrawal that can extend into the next couple of weeks. No wonder 95% of folks who attempt quitting with pure willpower end up throwing in the towel. They keep poking the mousetrap, telling themselves they'll outsmart it.

That's also why the idea of tapering off or planning to "only drink on weekends" is risky. You're always reintroducing the substance, forcing the body to re-adapt each time it thinks it's free. The daily or regular reintroduction ensures the mental cravings and physical symptoms never fully vanish. "Just one glass" resets the countdown, whether you planned to have that glass or not.

Granted, there are some situations—particularly for people consuming very large amounts daily—where quitting cold turkey can be physically dangerous, leading to severe effects such as seizures or delirium tremens. If you suspect you might be in that category, consult a medical professional. They can prescribe something to cushion those harsh withdrawal symptoms. That's not a sign of weakness; it's basic self-preservation. But for many, detoxing from a moderate-to-high level can be navigable if they're prepared for that short period of discomfort—and if they fortify themselves with the right supplements, knowledge, and support.

Which brings me to the next major point: once you stop drinking, we don't just leave you alone in the ring with your brain chemistry. We want to sabotage the "mental meltdown" that can occur when you feel edgy or anxious after day two or three. That's where certain supplements become powerful allies.

Let me be crystal clear: I'm not a doctor, and you should run any new supplement plan past your healthcare provider. This is especially important if you're on medications or have underlying conditions. But in my view, many folks—especially those who've battered their bodies with booze—need more nutrients than a typical mass-market multivitamin can offer. Here's a list of recommended additions that can ease the path out of alcohol dependency:

Omega-3 Capsules (1000 mg)

The human brain thrives on essential fats like EHA and DHA. They support neurotransmitter function, help regulate mood, and generally keep your mental machinery humming. Alcohol, unfortunately, is exceptionally good at destroying essential fats in your cells—like a harsh solvent that rips through protective layers and leaves them vulnerable. Most heavy drinkers, by definition, are lacking in these crucial fats. Replenishing them can be a game-changer for your emotional equilibrium and mental clarity.

Please skip the cod liver oil variety, as it's overloaded with vitamin A, which can cause problems if you also add other supplements into the mix. Instead, buy a dedicated, high-quality omega-3 supplement labeled with EHA and DHA content.

B Vitamin Complex

If you're a heavy drinker, you almost certainly have a B-vitamin deficiency, specifically B12. Alcohol not only depletes this vitamin, but can hamper your body's ability to absorb and use it. B12 supports everything from red blood cell formation to neurological function to DNA synthesis. Deficiency can cause a whole array of issues, from fatigue and constipation to depression-like symptoms. And in our quest for a stable mood, B12 is an asset in producing the "feel good" neurochemicals like serotonin and dopamine.

Sure, your multi might have some B12 in it, but likely not enough to refill your reserves. So it's wise to grab a separate B12 or B Complex supplement. The difference in your energy, mood, and concentration can be profound once you correct that deficiency.

Vitamin D

Many of us, especially in cooler climates or those glued to desks all day, are deficient in vitamin D. Some scientists don't even classify it as a vitamin anymore but as a hormone, given its wide-ranging effects on bone health, immune function, and even mood. A deficiency can leave you listless, sluggish, and prone to all sorts of health troubles. Although your multivitamin might list vitamin D, it's typically a fraction of the amount that leading experts recommend.

I'm not here to prescribe your dose, but I can share that some practitioners suggest around 20 IU per pound of body weight daily. For example, a 180-pound person would target around 3,600 IU daily. The older, outdated RDA is far too low to address the serious deficits many of us face. If you notice improved energy or a lift in your overall well-being after supplementing for a few weeks, that might be the sign you needed that you were low in D for a while.

But there's a catch: if you're taking a high dose of D, you should also consider vitamin K2, because these two vitamins work hand in hand for calcium transport and arterial health. Without K2, you might end up misplacing calcium in places it doesn't belong.

Magnesium

Magnesium is crucial for more than 300 biochemical reactions in your body, from maintaining stable blood pressure to aiding muscle and nerve function. Many heavy drinkers are magnesium-deficient without realizing it. That can lead to issues like insomnia, muscle cramps, or even irritability. You'll find some magnesium in your multivitamin, but it might be minimal, so topping up with a separate supplement is often wise. Also, combining magnesium with your vitamin D is beneficial, as magnesium helps your body convert that sunshine vitamin into a form it can use effectively.

If you do choose a magnesium supplement, check the label for forms like magnesium citrate or glycinate—they're considered more bioavailable than some cheaper forms.

Curcumin

This might seem like an odd addition, but research suggests that curcumin, the active component in turmeric, can protect the liver from certain forms of damage and reduce inflammation. Some studies on rodents with high-fat, high-alcohol diets found that curcumin prevented the suppression of certain protective enzymes in the liver. In simpler terms: it might help your body handle the aftereffects of alcohol usage, especially if your consumption has been high for years.

Of course, these findings come mostly from animal studies, so consider them as indicative but not conclusive. Still, if your liver has taken a beating, adding a curcumin supplement to your regimen might provide some measure of protection. Just make sure to pick a curcumin product designed for high bioavailability—ordinary turmeric powder passes through your system too quickly.

The reported benefits aren't limited to hepatic function. Some individuals report reduced joint pain or better overall inflammation control when they take a consistent dose of a well-formulated curcumin supplement. That can be a boon if your joints or immune system are somewhat battered after years of heavy drinking.

It's easy to balk at a list of eight or nine items. You might worry about the cost, or fear you'll be swallowing an entire handful of pills each morning. But remember, these supplements are bridging the gap left by years of toxic chemical intake. You'll be saving far more than what you spend, especially if you consider how expensive alcohol can get over the long run. Also, many find that once their body recovers, they can pare down their regimen to a smaller set of essentials. For now, though, I'd suggest you treat your system to a thorough overhaul.

But let me address a crucial point: you might wonder, "If I'm still physically dependent, shouldn't I wait until I'm sober to start supplements?" Generally, you can start them right away—though obviously check with your doctor first. Some, like vitamin C or a basic multivitamin, are safe for virtually everyone at recommended doses. Others, like high-dose vitamin D or 5-HTP, require a bit more caution. The key is to ensure you don't inadvertently create a new problem while trying to solve an existing one. That's precisely why I keep harping on about consulting your healthcare professional.

One last cautionary note about supplementation: watch out for your own lies about "miracle cures." None of these pills or capsules is a silver bullet that singlehandedly ends your addiction. They are more like scaffolding, helping your body recover from the havoc that long-term drinking can create. They ease withdrawal, support your mood, and reduce the likelihood that you'll get blindsided by crippling fatigue or depression during those first few vulnerable weeks. The actual decision to remain sober must still come from your own conviction that alcohol is no friend. If you keep telling yourself you'll eventually "drink in moderation," your mind can sabotage your best efforts.

So, how do we piece this all together into a coherent plan? Let's outline a hypothetical scenario:

Consult a Doctor

If you exhibit severe withdrawal symptoms—intense trembling, hallucinations, or seizures—seek medical help. They might prescribe something to buffer your detox, ensuring it doesn't become life-threatening.

Monitor Changes

Keep a simple journal of how you feel physically and mentally. Are your moods more stable? Is your sleep improving? Are you experiencing any abnormal side effects or interactions? Jot them down and discuss them with your doctor if anything seems off. Also note that if your emotional state is precarious, or if you feel you might relapse, seeking therapy or a support group is wise. Supplements can't do everything.

Be Realistic about the Kick

Even with these supplements, you'll have a period of unease. Some days you might wake up anxious for no clear reason. Recognize it's your body adapting to life without alcohol. Resist the temptation to interpret it as a "sign" you need a drink. If you hold steady, the unease will diminish as your brain recalibrates. The entire ordeal is often far shorter and gentler than the horror stories you may have heard. But the precise timeline varies from person to person.

Remember Why You're Doing This

Keep at the forefront of your mind all the reasons you decided to quit. Maybe it's the money you're saving, or the improved health, or the relationships you want to restore. Maybe you're just sick of the lies you've been telling yourself. Write those reasons down, stick them on your refrigerator, or set them as a note on your phone. The moment you're tempted to rationalize "just one glass," remind yourself it leads you back into the same cycle. The two-week clock restarts, and you lose momentum. That's a hefty price for a fleeting taste.

Plan for Potential Pitfalls

Are you invited to a wedding next week, or a social gathering where drinks flow freely? Don't let it blindside you. Think ahead. You might decide to arrive late, or leave early if you start feeling vulnerable. Or bring your own non-alcoholic beverage, so you're not stuck with a glass of water while others brandish cocktails. Some folks pre-load with a hearty meal or extra vitamins that day to keep themselves physically strong. Arm yourself with coping strategies. A sober buddy or an exit plan can be a lifesaver. If you see a queue forming at the bar, head outside for fresh air and a quick mental reset. The point is to avoid stumbling into a high-risk scenario unprepared.

Forgive Yourself if Slips Happen

In an ideal world, you'll put the bottle down and never pick it up again. But if you do slip, don't declare total defeat. The knowledge you've gained remains in your head. A relapse might mean you still harbor illusions about alcohol's "benefits." Revisit the illusions, dissect them, reaffirm your reasons for quitting, and re-commit. Supplements remain vital if you found them helpful earlier. The key is to stand back up swiftly. Don't give your ego the satisfaction of a meltdown that extends your binge.

If you find yourself picking up this text feeling skeptical about the supplement route—thinking it's too expensive or too complicated—I'd remind you that you've likely spent far more money on alcohol each week, month, and year than you'd ever spend on a handful of vitamins. The net result is that you can reallocate that "drinking budget" into something that helps you heal. It's a bargain in every sense. And once you're beyond the initial adjustments, your daily life might require just a few of these to keep your health on track.

By now, you might be thinking that never again letting a single drop pass your lips for two entire weeks is unthinkable. That's your addiction speaking, the illusions you've cultivated for so long. Once you have that clean period behind you—especially if you supplement to smooth the way—you'll see that the cravings can recede, the twitchiness can settle. Some might experience minor anxiety or insomnia in the first few days, but that's precisely why our recommended supplements include ones that support rest and mood, from magnesium to 5-HTP to B vitamins. They collectively act like scaffolding around you while you rebuild your life free from alcohol.

Another question that arises frequently is, "If I do all these steps, will I be absolutely guaranteed a quick and painless process?" The answer is no. There are no absolute guarantees in life, especially with something as multifaceted as addiction. Some people breeze through the initial fortnight, while others find it more challenging. Even identical twins can have dramatically different experiences due to personal stress levels, environment, or genetics. But giving your body the right nutrients can reduce the odds of a meltdown. Ultimately, you still need to keep your mind on the bigger goal: living a vibrant, free existence instead of numbing yourself each evening.

Since I'm emphasizing the nutritional angle quite heavily, let me also mention the role of a healthy diet. If you've been pounding your liver with booze daily, your body is starved for real nourishment. Incorporate more wholesome foods—lean proteins, fresh vegetables, fruits, whole grains—so your system has building blocks for recovery. The combination of a decent diet plus the supplements can accelerate your bounce back. Some folks even discover renewed interest in cooking, now that they're not half-drunk each night. That can be a lovely bonus.

Let's not forget about emotional triggers, either. While your brain's chemistry is recalibrating, emotions can run higher than usual. It's normal to feel restless or edgy at random times. A stable supply of vitamins, minerals, and essential fatty acids can help buffer these mood swings, but you should also think about stress management. That might mean taking up yoga, journaling your daily ups and downs, going for evening walks, or even trying guided meditation. If you feel out of your depth, a counselor or support group can guide you through emotional riptides.

Overall, I want to highlight that while the withdrawal period can be a jolt to the system, it's also your body's way of saying, "I'm rebalancing—stand by." You might interpret it as an unwavering sign that you're on the right path. That sense of mild discomfort or shakiness is the last stand of your addicted physiology. The more you reinforce your defenses with well-chosen supplements, the better you'll handle that shift. Before long, you'll notice that daily life feels more stable, your mind less foggy, your emotions more grounded. You'll rediscover a version of yourself that doesn't revolve around swirling a glass of something that smells pungent and tastes even worse if you dare to sample it without the illusions.

At the risk of sounding repetitive, all these suggestions hinge on your decision to break the loop fully. If you're still telling yourself you can return to "normal drinking," these steps might reduce your immediate withdrawal but won't uproot the delusions that keep you tethered. It's vital to commit, from deep inside, that you're done letting a sedative chemical rule your nights, your weekends, or your entire identity. Supplements simply grease the wheels for that transformation.

In summary, yes, it's possible to navigate the early days of sobriety with less misery than you might fear. Yes, the suite of recommended vitamins, oils, and minerals can drastically reduce the bumpy ride. No, you won't need them forever, though some, like vitamin D or omega-3, might become lifelong allies. And yes, you must still do the mental work—recognizing lies, setting boundaries, and holding firm when social pressures tempt you to "relax." If you do all this, you'll likely find that the dreaded "kick" is more of a short-lived inconvenience than a paralyzing odyssey. That's the best news of all: once you see through alcohol's false promises, the departure from it can be gentler than you imagined. You'll begin to reclaim the clarity, health, and happiness that was always your birthright—just hidden behind a swirl of alcohol-laced illusions.

Chapter 14: Controlling the Evil Clown

It might seem at first glance that you've reached some sort of "solution zone" within these pages. There's a temptation to skip ahead, latch on to a few quick tips, and then head off with a newly purchased bundle of vitamins under your arm. That approach may be understandable, but it's precisely the sort of short-circuiting that often derails any honest attempt to quit drinking. My method has multiple elements, each of which interlocks with the rest—so if you're tempted to hop straight to the end and cherry-pick the so-called cure, do yourself a favor and pause. All six steps play a role here, and you can't just do half of them and expect everything to click into place.

When you reflect on it, it's not surprising. This problem we're tackling is, after all, no small headache. We're contending with an ingrained pattern of behavior, shaped by countless beliefs and social cues, enforced by your own stubborn brain chemistry. Of course it's going to take more than a single tactic or pill. The earlier parts of this book serve to reframe your entire view of alcohol and show why it's not just a harmless social lubricant or a convenient stress reliever, but a cunningly disguised addictive depressant. If that shift in thinking hasn't happened for you yet, the next steps aren't going to do much good.

Nevertheless, let's assume you're here having already accepted that the daily glass (or three) is no innocent pastime. You recognize that the illusions can be dismantled, and you're actively dismantling them. If you want to boost your success rate, you'll need the synergy of all the steps, not just the handful that feel simplest. That synergy can't happen if you skip large chunks of the method. Even if you followed five of the six steps, I still couldn't guarantee success. Each piece is carefully designed to feed into the others. And if you've been with me since the start, you'll know by now that step one was basically crossing the threshold that says: "I'm done ignoring this problem; it's time to fix it." Step two was all about exposing the illusions. You learned to see alcohol for what it genuinely is, rather than what the marketing world or your own wishful thinking told you.

Maybe you still can't quite believe you've committed to this. Or perhaps you're feeling anxious, suspecting something else is on the horizon because you're worried that taking vitamins alone can't possibly cut it. If that's you, breathe easy. Vitamins and supplements are helpful, but they're not the entire formula. Picture it like baking a cake: you need flour, eggs, sugar, maybe cocoa if you're me. Leaving out even one ingredient can leave you with a sad, flat pancake, or something that tastes like raw chalk. Alcohol recovery is similar: skipping even one piece of the puzzle reduces your odds of success.

If you remain skeptical of the more intangible parts of this method—like the perspective shifts or the mindfulness tasks—that might be precisely the area you need the most. We can't rely on "I'll just do the bits that sound easiest." That's a sure path to partial results or outright failure.

It helps to map out what's happened so far in these pages. The first step was already in motion before you even opened the cover: acknowledging that something about your drinking isn't right. A lot of people remain stuck in denial. They know deep down that alcohol has seized too large a slice of their life, but they'll do anything to avoid confronting it. They'll shrug, "I only drink socially," or "Everyone around me does the same." Meanwhile, nights are lost, finances strangled, relationships eroded. The day you said "enough" was the real step one.

Then step two: reconceptualizing alcohol. This might be the hardest mental leap—convincing yourself that alcohol is not your ally, that it doesn't truly taste wonderful or ease stress or bring you joy. If you've reached this point but still maintain even a shred of "But I like the taste, and maybe just a small bit can't hurt," do yourself a big favor and return to the earlier chapters. Revisit all the reasons that line of thinking is a booby-trap. Because the illusions run deeply. If you cling to the notion that alcohol provides some unique benefit, it's practically impossible to let go. It's like trying to stop hugging a cactus while whispering, "But it's so comforting." Let me be blunt: if you're still half-believing there's a benefit, you're not going to make it far. You'll keep reaching for that glass because deep down you think it's your friend.

If, on the other hand, you've committed to the notion that drinking is basically self-sabotage, you're ready for the rest of the steps. You might even have that list of recommended supplements in your hand, and you're primed to use them. So let's suppose you have all the bits in place: your new understanding of alcohol, your vow that you see no advantage in further consumption, and your fresh stash of vitamins. At this juncture, we address one of the biggest hidden saboteurs: your ego's flair for predicting doom.

It's quite a showstopper, that ego. Even after everything we've discussed, it might pop up at random intervals, casting doubt on whether you can function at a party without a drink in hand, or whether you'll ever have a day of real relaxation if you give up the bottle. You might be in the car, daydreaming about a future scenario, and a voice says, "A dinner with old friends? That won't be any fun if I can't have a glass or two of wine." That's your ego speaking, weaving a story about the future that it can't possibly verify. Because the future doesn't exist yet—it's just a mental projection. The only real moment is now. If you learn to notice that phenomenon as it's happening—like a spectator acknowledging an actor on stage—you strip it of its potency. Otherwise, you might get carried along by the storyline, forgetting that it's pure speculation.

Sometimes the ego tries the same trick with the past. Perhaps you recall nights when you laughed with your buddies, believing the alcohol was at the core of that joy.

You might interpret that memory as proof that a sober future is dull. But a memory is also not reality; it's a curated, incomplete snippet of experience that might omit plenty of cringe-worthy details. The ego loves to rummage in old times to justify present cravings or to conjure anxiety about tomorrow.

This is why a huge part of the next step is about reconnecting with the present moment. The present moment is notoriously overshadowed by regrets about yesterday or concerns about tomorrow. Even seemingly positive thoughts like, "I can't wait to see my kids tonight," subtly imply that you're not fully satisfied with the now. The ego is always looking for ways to nudge you out of the present—either by stoking resentment over past injustices or by fueling worries or cravings about the future. For someone trying to stay sober, that's a hidden minefield. The mental chatter that arises can lead to catastrophizing about life without alcohol.

As I've mentioned, the solution isn't to fight your thoughts or guilt yourself for having them. Instead, you want to notice. Simply observe when your mind drifts off into anxious predictions or nostalgic fantasies about your old drinking habit. With a slight smile, think, "There's the ego again, pretending it can see what hasn't happened or recall the past as if it's a living truth." That observation alone can help break the chain of illusions. The more you anchor yourself in the actual now—focusing on your breath, your immediate surroundings, or the sensation in your limbs—the less sway the ego has.

I've known people who balk at this approach, thinking it must be more complicated. But ironically, the best solutions often are quite simple, though not necessarily easy. The same mind that invented a labyrinth of lies about alcohol can't be forced to change with brute willpower. It tends to respond better when you gently disarm it by refusing to take its drama too seriously. The ego says, "Next month is going to be a disaster without cocktails!" and you respond, "Well, I don't actually know what next month holds. I might discover something even more fun." All you have to do is recognize that the future doesn't exist yet, so letting your mind fill it with doomsday scenarios is pointless.

If you think that's too woo-woo, consider how you feel in the midst of daydreaming about future tensions. You might get an elevated heart rate, sweaty palms, or a general sense of dread, all from pictures in your head. Next time you notice yourself going down that spiral, try focusing on something tangible—such as counting your breaths or listening for distant sounds. Do it for 60 seconds. Many find that tension abates, partly because they've reclaimed the present. Doing that consistently can transform the emotional landscape of your day.

I often reference some classic tips for living in the moment. One trick is to catch yourself making predictions that revolve around negativity. If you picture a party you're about to attend and your brain says, "This is going to be awkward, I'll feel left out," realize that's purely an invention. It might or might not be accurate. You can't know. Since the moment is still in the future, you can't rely on your predictions. The more you see how unreliable your mind is at prophesying, the less you'll let it run wild. And if you train yourself to keep eyes on the now, you bypass half of the pitfalls that lead people to relapse.

A sense of humor helps here, too. Next time you catch your mind drifting into the past or forging an elaborate scenario about the future, you can give a gentle smirk, as though you're watching a ridiculous infomercial promising you the moon. "Thanks, mind," you might think, "I see you're up to your usual theatrics." The more you can see it as comedic—like a silly puppet show—the easier it is to ignore. Because the deeper truth is that those delusions only control you if you take them at face value.

I realize we're diving deep into a realm that might seem less "practical" than "buy these supplements." But trust me, the mental dimension is arguably the biggest factor. You can chug every vitamin on the planet, but if your ego successfully drags you into meltdown each time you imagine a future event without booze, you'll be in trouble. So this step of noticing the ego's attempts to hijack your thinking is critical.

One advantage is that once you train yourself to spot these beliefs, you might see improvements in other spheres of life, not just sobriety. Maybe you handle stress at work better, or you get less rattled when someone cuts you off in traffic. That's because the same mechanism is at play: your mind leaps ahead or rummages through the past, stirring up upset feelings, and you learn to call it out. Over time, you'll find you spend less energy fighting battles that don't exist outside your imagination.

You might ask, "Is it even possible to always live in the present?" or "Isn't some planning for the future necessary?" Sure, you need to plan. But planning is different from anxious predictions or illusions about how certain events must unfold. Good planning is mindful, purposeful, and then you come back to what you're doing right now. Unproductive fretting is like a skipping record that never reaches resolution. That's what the ego loves—setting you up to stress about something intangible, leading you back to the comfort of a drink or the alcohol of wishing you could fast-forward time.

I sometimes share stories of how even small triggers can sabotage a day. Perhaps you put on an outfit you haven't worn in a while and realize it's too tight. Instantly, your mind is off to the races: "I've put on weight. I'm letting myself go. My partner might not find me attractive." It's a chain of assumptions that spiral into fear. In that moment, you might be only too keen to pour a glass of something to dull the sense of shame. Again, illusions. All that anxiety is merely your ego conjuring a storyline about how the future must be painful. But if you catch it, you might realize that, hey, you can pick a different outfit, or you can calmly note you'd like to eat healthier. The difference is the emotional meltdown is optional.

Back to alcohol specifically: the illusions can be even more intense. You might wonder how you'll survive major holidays or celebrations. You might think of all the events you used to attend with a glass in hand. The mind leaps in to declare, "That party's going to be excruciating. Everyone else will be happily sipping away, and I'll be a bored outcast." Yet you can't know that. It's guesswork, fueled by the stories you used to believe about how essential alcohol is to enjoying yourself. If you step up, attend the event with an open mind and a few coping strategies (like a favorite non-alcoholic beverage), you might discover you laugh just as much, or even more. Or that you truly can't abide half the conversation that you used to find hilarious only because you were hammered. So you might come away realizing you prefer smaller, more genuine gatherings. That's not a tragedy; it's clarity. The point is your future enjoyment is not set in stone, and the only way to find out is to remain present enough to discover real life rather than let illusions chase you back to the bottle.

There's a quote I enjoy referencing: "If you worry about what might be, and wonder what might have been, you'll ignore what is." That's the heart of step four. Just observe how many times a day your mind tries to yank you into a time warp—either backward or forward—and see if you can gently decline the invitation. Resist the urge to label those thoughts as "bad." They're just thoughts. Smile at them, let them drift, and return to the now. Rinse and repeat. Over time, you'll realize you're less frequently sideswiped by cravings that revolve around fantasizing about "needing" a drink in a hypothetical future scenario.

If, for example, you start to panic about the upcoming family wedding in three months, that's a perfect moment to apply this method. Laugh at the urge to stress. You can't predict how you'll feel in three months. You might be in an even better place than you are now. Then you exhale, ground yourself in the present, and keep going with your day. You'll handle that wedding when you arrive at it. Maybe you'll find new ways to be sociable, or maybe you'll spot that the real reason you used to "need" a drink at these events was social anxiety. In that case, you can actively tackle the anxiety instead of doping it with booze.

There's no universal prescription for how to handle every future challenge, but you do have a universal tool in your back pocket: remain anchored in what's happening right now. That might mean noticing the sights and sounds around you, zeroing in on your breathing, or simply focusing on your bodily sensations. People often find that the moment they do that, a wave of calm emerges. Because in the now, you rarely have the dire catastrophes your mind conjures. You're simply living, breathing, and reading, or working, or cooking, or walking. That's not so scary.

There might also be times your mind conjures a pleasant future scenario—like how you can't wait for next summer's beach holiday, anticipating the sandy toes and the warm sun. Even then, your ego is subtly reminding you that happiness must be somewhere else in time, not here. That's not necessarily a big negative, but if you pile enough of those illusions together, you spend all your moments living in a world that doesn't exist yet, missing out on real-time existence. And ironically, that's one of the key triggers for wanting a drink: you keep pining for states of mind that are anywhere but your present. The alcohol you get from a glass can mimic the idea of "escape."

But genuine escape from illusions is far more satisfying than alcohol. Once you experience that for a few weeks, you might find you have no real desire to return to the old pattern. That's where synergy of steps is so crucial. Step one was your initial admission that something needed to change. Step two was clarifying the lies around alcohol. Step three involved adding the right supplements to support your body's transition. Now, step four is about defanging the ego's beliefs of future or past. Steps five and six will build on that, reinforcing your determination not to slip back.

If you're still feeling a twinge of "This is too easy," remember you might be falling for the typical trap of the mind: expecting a torturous approach to be the only real solution. People sometimes want a dramatic, tear-filled confrontation with their addiction, complete with a near-death experience. In truth, the best transformations can happen quietly, with a lot of gentle daily awareness. Breaking illusions doesn't require a meltdown; it requires consistent noticing and re-centering. Hardly glamorous, but highly effective.

Some might think it sounds suspiciously like certain spiritual philosophies: mindfulness, present-moment awareness, that sort of thing. They're not wrong. A big chunk of reprogramming your brain after an addiction is to calm that swirl of mental predictions. Many spiritual traditions talk about the tyranny of time-based thinking, and you're seeing the practical reason why. Once you see how it colludes with addiction, you realize this is not some airy-fairy concept. It has real, tangible consequences for daily sobriety.

I suggest you give yourself 21 days—like a self-imposed experiment—to practice living more in the moment, noticing illusions of the past or future, and returning your focus to the present whenever possible. You might be shocked at the difference in your mental clarity after just three weeks. Or you might find it initially frustrating but eventually see pockets of relief from your old patterns. Either outcome is progress. Even a little improvement in quieting the delusions can have ripple effects on your confidence in staying sober.

As part of this experiment, you could keep a small daily log. Not a big journaling project, just a line or two each night: "Noticed the mind worrying about next week's get-together; recognized it was an ego prediction. Came back to focusing on my breathing." No big lecture to yourself, just a quick note. Then you watch how these small noticings add up over time. You might see that your old triggers pop up less often, and when they do, they're less potent.

People often ask, "What if I slip?" The same principle applies. A slip is typically triggered by illusions about how you "need" a drink to handle a moment or about how "one glass never hurt anyone." Reflect on it, see the illusions that preceded it, and carry on. The real damage is done when you magnify a slip into a meltdown about how you're doomed to fail forever. That meltdown is nothing more than predictions again, lies about tomorrow.

All of this might feel like a big shift from the earlier parts of the book, where we dissected the chemical mechanics of alcohol withdrawal and a laundry list of supplements. But hopefully you can see how it ties together seamlessly. If you combine the attitude that alcohol is worthless with the right nutritional support, plus the skill of defusing illusions about time, you're forging a robust foundation for permanent sobriety.

The next two steps build even further, but only if you give step four a good shot. I can't stress this enough: skipping the present-moment approach is like building a tall tower on shaky ground. The beliefs about the future are what often drive cravings. It's the worry that you'll never enjoy birthdays, never handle stress, never sleep well. If you allow your mind to run with those illusions unchecked, it has a secret passage back to the bottle. The present-moment technique is your guard at the gate. Each time the illusions approach with a sob story, you notice them, politely decline to engage, and remain in the real world. Over time, the illusions see there's no easy route in, and they quiet down.

One final mention: if you do the 21-day presence challenge with real intent, you might realize that the lies aren't limited to drinking. You'll notice them creeping up in every corner of life—relationships, work, self-esteem, finances. That's normal. The same mental patterns that fed your alcohol addiction probably feed other anxieties or regrets. This awareness helps you address them all. A nice side effect of stopping drinking is that you might find other issues in your life start to improve as well, as you become less bogged down by delusions or time-based negativity.

So let's step off the stage with that understanding. When your mind leaps to "Will I cope at that future event?" or "I messed up that thing last year," see it for what it is: a mental reel playing illusions about a time that isn't real right now. Smile at it, let it drift by, and refocus on the now. Repeat as needed. Yes, it takes practice and patience, but the payoff is significant. And if you're determined to live a life free from of alcohol, your mind at peace, and your body no longer battered by daily toxins, this is the pivot that can make it all possible.

Chapter 15: Dealing With the Kick

Sometimes there's a sudden transformation, almost like a light turning on. You wake up one morning and realize the taste of wine you found so delightful yesterday now seems decidedly stale. You figure you must have changed your mind about alcohol, and you don't see much reason to keep drinking. For a lot of people, that's the end of the road—no drama, no fuss. They just think, "I'd rather not," and they're done.

But for others, it might be a slower burn. Even though you understand, logically, that there's nothing left to gain from booze, there's a period where this information needs time to settle in and become a genuine, unshakeable conviction. You wander around the house, noticing small details you never observed before: a certain brand of whiskey you used to enjoy, or the empty bottles sitting in the recycling bin. You might start seeing your friends in a different light when they're on their third or fourth glass at a party. They stand there, with the rosy glow that used to seem enviable but now looks more like alcohol. You can see them slur their words, repeating the same silly anecdote while believing they're the life and soul of the evening. You wonder how you missed that behavior for years. But it's easy to miss—everyone around them is also in a haze, so it all seems normal. When you step outside that haze, you realize how odd the scene can appear.

At around the same time, you start noticing how the alcohol industry relentlessly tries to glamorize the product you're rethinking. Watch an ad with a newly critical eye: the bouncy music, the young, attractive actors, and the faintly sexual vibe that underpins it all. You see the brand implying, "Drink this, and you'll be desirable," or, "Pop this cork, and your house party transforms into an upscale dream." And it dawns on you that the entire spectacle is less about refreshment and more about hooking into primal urges like sex and belonging. This is hardly news. Advertisers have used sexuality for over a century to shift everything from shampoo to hamburgers. But with alcohol, it's not just a marketing ploy—it's the illusion that can lead you back into an addictive loop if you're not careful.

There's a longstanding theory that a part of our brain is basically reptilian, governed by fundamental drives such as hunger, thirst, reproduction. The link between booze and sex is tenuous at best—beer ads might show a sweaty guy with chiseled abs, or a bikini-clad model laughing at a dumb joke, but there's no chemical reason to pair them except that, well, people respond to sexual imagery. The marketing world is happy to exploit that link, however flimsy, because it works. Men have been known to switch brand loyalty on a dime if a commercial features an attractive model in a provocative pose. Women aren't immune either: a dashing man with a crooked smile can conjure up all sorts of fantasies. So the next time you see those carefully airbrushed characters winking at you from a billboard, remember they're there for one reason: to snag your reptilian brain.

Meanwhile, the real truth about how alcohol actually affects sexuality is more sobering. It's not a beacon of confidence or allure. In fact, you might recall the first time you kissed a drunken partner while you yourself were stone-cold sober. The best word to describe that moment might have been stale or sour. A mind fogged by alcohol is rarely an appealing partner; the supposed wonders of a "drunk kiss" or "drunk fun" are illusions that crumble the second you stand outside of it. So the idea that a glass of brand X or a bottle of brand Y magically leads to steamy nights or heroic social prowess is just that—marketing spin, repeated endlessly until it's as familiar as a lullaby.

You see your colleagues at the end of a workday sigh with relief at the mention of "that first drink to unwind." You know enough now to recognize the real dynamic: after eight hours away from last night's alcohol, they're mid-withdrawal. Their body is crying out for alcohol to calm the mild anxiety that arises as the blood loses the drug from the previous round. The moment they sip that wine, the tension disappears. So they assume it's relaxing them, but in truth, it's just removing the mild agitation that alcohol introduced in the first place. If you didn't drink last night, you're not going to feel that creeping sense of stress. You can see it plainly once you stand on the outside of the ritual: they're chasing peace, but ironically, they're chasing the relief from symptoms they inflicted on themselves the evening before.

By the time you've recognized these beliefs, you might have already embarked on your "two weeks of no drinking," that window where physical withdrawal subsides a little more each day. With every 24-hour block, the craving or sense of restlessness shrinks. If you haven't caved and resumed drinking, you're on track to let your body rebalance. Maybe you're also following the advice about supplements, which can be a cushion for your nervous system. It's not always a quick fix; some people notice a dramatic boost in mood and energy in a week, others require a month or more to see the shift. Some don't notice anything until they momentarily stop taking them—and realize how much they were helping.

Of course, you may still get blindsided by a strong urge to have a drink, so overwhelming it feels like your mind is screaming for immediate alcohol. In those intense moments, it can help to recall a technique called Thought Field Therapy (TFT). Although it might seem like something from a New Age festival, thousands attest to its efficacy for cravings and phobias. It involves tapping on specific meridian points on the upper body, akin to a simplified acupuncture practice without needles. The idea is to intercept the "program" in your brain that's commanding you to drink, just as you'd do Ctrl+Alt+Delete on a misbehaving computer. You might raise an eyebrow at the concept, but the proof is in how many people find it useful. If tapping your cheekbones or the space above your eyebrow for a few seconds can stop a meltdown, it's certainly worth a try. Surrender your skepticism for a moment, Google it, and you'll find countless testimonials. Personally, I view it as a handy fire extinguisher. You might not need it every day, but you'll be grateful it's there if the flames appear.

You might also find yourself having vivid dreams about drinking. Don't be rattled if you wake up half-convinced you were guzzling down a bottle of beer or opening a fancy Cabernet. Such dreams are normal. They're your brain's way of sifting through the big changes in your life. Dreams feed on what occupies our thoughts. If you watch a spy movie before bed, you might dream of outrunning shadowy villains. Similarly, if you've spent all day focusing on sobriety, your subconscious might weave that theme into your nighttime storylines. These dreams aren't a sign you're failing or that you secretly desire to drink. They're merely your internal drama department playing out the day's anxieties. If you keep noticing them, try to greet each one with a wry smile. It's a good sign, in a twisted sense, because it means your mind is actively processing the shift.

Another odd phenomenon might be a sense of mild sadness in situations where you once would have had a drink. Picture yourself on holiday, for instance. If you used to see vacations as an all-day pass to drink from sunup to sundown, your first sober trip might feel a bit strange. You stroll by the pool around 10 a.m., the time you'd typically pop open a can of lager, and you're holding a soft drink instead. It can produce an eerie sense of something missing. Not a longing to be hammered, but a vaguely disorienting emptiness. That's just your conditioned habit raising its eyebrows and murmuring, "Are you sure you're not forgetting something?"

I recall a holiday scenario of my own when I first quit. My wife (at the time) and I arrived in Cyprus. Our old routine included rolling out of bed, sipping on something alcoholic before noon, and continuing until bedtime. Suddenly, that routine was gone. One evening, we entered a bar we'd visited many times, run by a friendly Greek Cypriot named Andreas. He recognized us instantly, whisked us to a perfect table, and chatted warmly about how nice it was to see us back. Moments later, the barmaid appeared with a tray: a glass of wine for my wife, playful mocktails for the children, and, for me, a cold beer. Andreas smiled with pride, certain he'd remembered our old favorites. This was precisely the moment I realized I had no plan for politely refusing it. I ended up discreetly dumping the beer into a nearby plant pot (poor plant) and requesting a soda. I wasn't resentful of my wife's wine, nor did I envy her. The faint sadness was more the abrupt recognition that I was in a place once intimately linked with my drinking, and that link was now severed. It felt like wearing someone else's shoes—no urgent pain, just a sense of not belonging. But over the next few days, I realized it was simply a new reality. The "holiday me" no longer needed to revolve around an endless parade of cocktails.

You may find similarly jarring moments at weddings or big social events where free champagne is offered in trays. You might think, "But, but… it's a wedding." The notion that refusing a free drink is somehow taboo. Or maybe you feel that nudge of sadness. If that hits you, it's a sign of conditioning, nothing more. A part of you believes some crucial piece of your experience is absent, even though you logically know you don't want that piece. It's exactly like adjusting from driving a stick shift for years to suddenly driving an automatic. Your muscle memory expects you to press a clutch pedal that isn't there. You'll try to shift gears, momentarily confused. But eventually, that weird feeling fades, and you adapt to the new environment. If you revert to your old manual car weeks later, you'll face another minor period of awkwardness. The key is to see all these mismatched feelings as signs that you're rewiring your reflexes.

You might wonder how long it will take until your sober self feels so automatic that you can't fathom how you ever did it differently. That, of course, varies. Some people flip the switch and find themselves comfortable in new routines within days. Others need multiple experiences—like traveling abroad, attending celebratory events, or even just hosting a small dinner—to retrain their mind that the old reflex of "I need a drink now" is no longer relevant. Over time, you might experience an ironic phenomenon: you'll wonder how you ever enjoyed the taste. You'll see a tipsy colleague at a work function, slurring words, thinking they're brilliant, and you'll be baffled that you ever found that appealing. So that seed you planted will keep sprouting. The illusions about how wonderful alcohol is keep unraveling each time you watch the alcohol from the outside.

It's worth mentioning that these illusions die hardest in spaces where everything is set up to remind you of your old habit. Maybe it's a bar in your hometown you used to frequent, or a kitchen table where you always placed your nightly glass of red. The environment can trigger a Pavlovian reaction. If you find yourself in that place unexpectedly, the memory might rush back with surprising force. The key is simply to notice, "Ah, that's my old autopilot flaring up," rather than interpret it as a genuine craving. Once you realize the difference, it loses much of its emotional weight.

If you do catch yourself feeling a pang of "loss," remind yourself: you're not missing something that actually enhanced your life. All you're missing is the psychological alcohol of a drug that left you tired, lighter in the wallet, and burdened with regretful mornings. That might quell the pang right away, or it might take a few attempts. The good news is, each time you reinforce your new perspective, you accelerate the process of rewriting the habit.

On a final note, you might encounter well-meaning or even pushy friends who claim you look sad or bored without your usual drink. Don't let them rewrite your narrative. If you do feel awkward or bored, it's not because you need alcohol; it's because you're shifting from autopilot to a new mode. Let them think what they will. If they push you to "loosen up," it's usually because your sober presence quietly challenges their lies. Resist the trap of justifying yourself or launching into a lecture. A simple, "I'm good, thanks," is enough. Over time, if they see you calm, enjoying the moment without alcohol, they might reevaluate who's truly missing out.

Yes, you may still stumble on the odd emotional pothole: that pang of strangeness in a holiday bar, that short wave of sadness at a lavish wedding. Recognize these for what they are—echoes of the old pattern, not real longing. Alcohol can't solve anything; it can only sedate you short-term while planting seeds for tomorrow's cravings. The more you see how thoroughly you were conned, the easier it is to remain free. And day by day, situation by situation, the unfamiliar eventually becomes your new normal.

Chapter 16: Questions!

You'd be amazed at how often I receive questions from people who see themselves as "problem drinkers" yet hope I'll confirm that they can keep drinking anyway. Some folks search for any excuse—any shred of good news that might offer permission to carry on swirling that glass. And let's be honest, the desire to find a loophole is completely understandable. Alcohol has been dressed up for decades as a glamorous social lubricant, a stress reliever, or an essential part of any celebration, so naturally, the idea of living without it can seem unnerving. But if you've reached the point of exploring this method, there's a good chance you see the illusions for what they are. That doesn't mean a million questions won't arise along the way.

Over the years, I've gathered a variety of queries that repeatedly crop up. The ones below might be rattling around in your own head right now, and I hope my responses will clarify some of the more persistent myths, anxieties, or misunderstandings.

First, though, do me a favor: as you read, remember the fundamental premise of this method. You don't have to keep searching for reasons to cling to alcohol once you recognize it's an attractively packaged poison. The devilish illusions that society sells us—convenient half-truths and marketing gimmicks—are formidable. They'll whisper that there's some magical hack to keep your habit "safe." But if you accept that the best solution is simply to remove alcohol from your life, these questions take on an entirely different tone. They become signposts on your journey away from alcohol, rather than potential excuses for you to revert to old patterns.

Q1: "I want to stop drinking, but my circle of friends is pretty intense. If I don't go out drinking with them, I'll never hear the end of it. Shouldn't I just cut back instead of giving up completely?"

It's not unusual to feel strong social pressure around alcohol. Culturally, many people connect heavy drinking with toughness or bravado. In some circles, you earn respect by showing how much you can "handle," as though building a tolerance to a toxic substance is some kind of admirable achievement. If you're worried your mates might start calling you names or making you the butt of jokes, welcome to the club. It's an unfortunate reality that many drinkers not only expect you to join them at the bar, they get quite threatened when you choose not to.

When I was still drinking, I had a reputation for being able to "keep up with the best of them." Oddly, that was treated like a badge of honor among the group I hung out with. Once I decided enough was enough, I stopped in November—a move that in my old mindset seemed preposterous because "nobody goes sober right before Christmas." That just highlights how deeply we're all conditioned. I used to think, "Better to wait until January," as though the calendar date mattered to the seriousness of my decision.

Shortly after I quit, I had to attend a holiday get-together with these same old pals. We settled into a pub. My friend Roy stepped up to the bar, ordered a pint of some potent imported beer, then looked at me with raised eyebrows and said, "Same again for you?" I calmly asked for a Diet Coke. He was speechless for a moment, then launched into, "A Coke? Don't be an idiot—man up, get a pint!" which quickly devolved into jibes about my masculinity, sexuality, or whatever else he could invoke to shame me. You might face a similar barrage. The delusions run deep, and the best way for them to keep illusions intact is to drag you back into the fold. But if you stand your ground—without anger, just calmly repeating that you're okay with your soda—they'll eventually move on to the next topic. In my case, Roy now orders me a Diet Coke automatically, though he'll likely still throw a playful insult about how I "turned soft." But it's just banter at this point. They will adapt, so hold firm.

Cutting down for the sake of pleasing your friends is a shaky plan. If you do that, you're still telling your subconscious that part of you believes alcohol is beneficial. That belief is precisely the crack in the door that beliefs need to creep back in. A partial approach is more vulnerable to collapse, whereas going all in on quitting can be oddly simpler. At least then your friends realize you're serious. It might take them time, but as they see your unwavering position, they'll start handing you your usual non-alcoholic beverage without blinking. Friendships can survive if they're built on something stronger than a shared addiction to alcohol.

Q2: "I read that milk thistle protects the liver. If I start taking it, can I keep drinking?"

That question is a prime example of looking for a pass to stay in the mousetrap. Milk thistle (Silybum marianum) is indeed touted as a remedy for liver issues, and some studies suggest it can help protect liver cells from toxins. However, the actual human research is inconsistent—some studies indicate a mild benefit, while others show a negligible effect. Even if it were conclusively proven that milk thistle could help shield your liver from moderate damage, does that justify continuing a habit that robs you of time, money, health, and mental clarity?

If you're at a point where you see alcohol is the root cause of all sorts of problems, relying on milk thistle is like wearing a plastic hat in a hailstorm. It might deflect a few pebbles, but the hail is still raining down. If anything, the idea that you can keep drinking because you've found a magical protective herb suggests you're still trying to justify the habit. Ask yourself if that logic is any different from the old "If I don't inhale, it won't hurt me" approach that some smokers used to adopt. The lies remain illusions. And besides, milk thistle won't fix the social, psychological, or financial issues that heavy drinking drags behind it.

Q3: "What about Christmas, Thanksgiving, and other big social occasions? How on earth do I skip drinking then?"

The easiest way to answer that question might be to ask, "How do you resist heroin at Christmas? Or a daily injection of meth?" Harsh analogy, right? But it's relevant. We don't typically crave heroin on holidays because we never believed it had any value for us. The same should be true for alcohol once you see it for the addictive depressant it is. If you still believe the illusions—that a family gathering or festive season requires you to get hammered—then that belief itself is your real hurdle, not the season or the event.

How we celebrate is culturally influenced. If you were living in a predominantly teetotal culture, would you still say, "How can I not drink at a wedding?" The answer is no, because the norms would be different, so you wouldn't assume that you need to mix poison with your celebrations. Even in Western traditions, the idea that Christmas or birthdays must revolve around booze is a fairly recent addition. It's not in the biblical story of the Nativity; the angels didn't pop open champagne to toast baby Jesus. That's entirely a modern overlay. The same goes for birthdays—some people throw lavish parties with zero alcohol, and guess what, they still have fun.

If you're genuinely worried about feeling left out, that implies you still think you're missing out on something precious. Remind yourself that you're not missing out on anything beneficial. You're avoiding alcohol. That's not a deprivation. If you remain unconvinced, keep returning to the illusions you once believed: that booze makes a holiday special or helps you unwind after a big meal. You know better now, so reaffirm that knowledge each time these old assumptions pop up. You might still sense a twinge of awkwardness, but with each holiday you spend sober, you gain clarity on how much more present you are with your loved ones, how many more vivid memories you're collecting, and how you're no longer dealing with that dreaded hangover the next morning.

Q4: "So, does your approach mean you think the spiritual angle of groups like AA is just nonsense?"

Not at all. In fact, the spiritual dimension can be profoundly effective for some individuals. Many people find that a connection to a higher power or a sense of divine presence helps them navigate emotional storms. My issue is that a lot of folks run away the moment they hear words like "God" or "spirit," especially if they're not religious. They might suspect it's some cult agenda. That fear can be enough to keep them from benefiting from potentially transformative principles. Some programs, like AA, revolve around the concept that you're powerless against alcohol and must lean on a higher power to reclaim sanity. If you're comfortable with that framework, great. If you're not, there are alternative paths. Either way, the actual power behind the spiritual side is acknowledging there's something bigger than your own ego. Sometimes letting go is the only way to break free from illusions you've carried for years.

I personally lean more on something known as Ho'oponopono—an ancient Hawaiian process focused on acceptance, forgiveness, and gratitude. It's rooted in the idea that you create your own reality and that by cleaning the negative patterns in your mind, you cleanse the external manifestations of them. It might sound far-fetched to some, but so does the notion that we'd voluntarily pay for a substance that leaves us hungover and depressed. If spirituality resonates with you—whether that's meditation, prayer, or chanting mantras—go for it. The ultimate point is to recognize that you are not your addiction. If faith or spiritual practice cements that understanding, more power to you.

Q5: "I'm happy to report I've quit drinking, but now I'm having these vivid dreams about alcohol every single night. Is this normal? And can I stop them from happening?"

Yes, it's normal, and no, you probably can't stop them, at least not immediately. Many people have an identical experience. They'll dream of slamming back shots, opening a bottle of wine, or stealthily sipping vodka from a hidden flask, and it feels so real that they wake up thinking they've actually done it. Some folks even leap out of bed to inspect their kitchen for empty bottles. The first few times, it can be pretty unsettling.

The reason for these dreams is twofold. First, your mind is essentially processing your new alcohol-free reality. During the day, you're focusing on all these new behaviors—declining drinks, ignoring illusions, maybe reading about sobriety. That content becomes fodder for your subconscious, which tinkers with it in dreamland. Second, your brain is adjusting to the absence of a substance to which it had grown accustomed. Alcohol, even in moderate amounts, affects your sleep cycles and your general neurochemistry. Once you remove it, your brain is a bit off-kilter for a while. Vivid dreams can be one quirk of that transition.

If you start to understand that these dreams are your mind's way of reorganizing information, you can shrug them off more easily. They're not evidence of failure or hidden craving. They're simply your mental operating system rebooting. Over time, they'll fade. Some might persist occasionally—perhaps once every few months you'll have a weird dream about a big binge—but you'll likely find they become less and less emotionally charged. You might even find them somewhat comedic: "There I was, hugging a giant whiskey bottle shaped like a cactus. I woke up, realized it was nonsense, and moved on."

The same shift in brain chemistry might also cause you to notice how artificially you used to knock yourself out at night. Alcohol is not a sleep aid; it's an anesthetic. "Sleeping" under the influence is more akin to a reversible coma, lacking the normal restorative qualities. When you cut out alcohol, your body can re-engage in genuine sleep patterns—though it might take a bit for those cycles to stabilize. Don't be surprised if you feel more awake in the mornings, even if you still dream about old drinking scenes. The difference is your dreams now reflect an active, healthy brain sorting through data, rather than a semi-comatose alcohol that blocks off normal REM cycles.

All of this is to say, dreaming about alcohol is not a sign you're on the wrong path. In fact, it might be a sign that your mind is working diligently to integrate your new sober perspective. As you keep walking this path, the dreams will likely fade, or if they occasionally pop up, you'll greet them with a sort of casual amusement. If anything, they'll highlight how far you've come.

So, if you happen to wake up sweaty from a weird booze dream, just remind yourself: it's a snippet of your subconscious storyline, not an omen. Plenty of people have experienced the same. It's one of those ephemeral side effects of the radical shift you've made in your life. And sure, it might freak you out the first few times, but once you see it for what it is, it loses its power to alarm you.

Q6. Can I ever return to drinking in moderation?

It's surprisingly common for many people to say they don't want to stop drinking completely—they just want to cut down. Maybe you're in that position yourself, wondering if moderation is the key, hoping you can fine-tune your habits so the aftermath isn't so destructive, but the pleasure remains. That might sound lovely in theory, but let's go beyond theory and consider reality. If you've arrived at the conclusion that your relationship with alcohol is out of control, it likely means you've tried moderation in all sorts of different guises, and it never really stuck. It's not your imagination, and there's a reason it feels like an endless exercise in futility. When someone's physiology and psychology are primed by dependency, attempts to "reduce" consumption typically yield more stress and guilt than genuine relief.

It's a bit like stepping into a mousetrap, then hoping to dodge the snap by standing on tiptoe. If the trap's loaded, your best move is to remove yourself completely. That's why

I often point out that the only logical solution is to exit the trap entirely. If you think about other drugs—pick something harsh like heroin—nobody would suggest you keep injecting heroin but in smaller amounts. The idea would sound downright absurd, yet with alcohol, we have this socially approved delusion that it's less savage a chemical, so maybe partial usage can be just fine. But if you've been orbiting the problem of daily drinking or bingeing, it means your lies have been tested by real life, and beliefs tend to fail the stress test every time.

You might take a while to decide you've truly had enough, and that's all right. We can't force that inner conviction out of nowhere. It has to rise up from within. Sometimes you read a book like this multiple times or gather enough experiences that confirm moderation is a mirage. Eventually, it clicks: "No matter how I tinker with my drinking, I end up back where I started." A friend once told me, "I can limit my drinks for a few days, but it's like riding a wave—eventually, I wipe out on the shore and wash up with an empty bottle in hand." If you can relate, that's your sign that you can't safely stick to half measures.

Don't beat yourself up if you're still in the stage of thinking you can control it. You aren't alone. My online stop-drinking community is packed with folks who repeatedly tried "only on weekends," or "just wine, never vodka," or "strictly with food," and so on. The illusions are endless, and we want to cling to them because it's painful to imagine losing something we falsely believe has a benefit. There's that famous line about how you can't be "a little bit pregnant" – the condition is either on or off. Alcoholism is like that too. Even if you manage a brief period of partial success at limiting intake, the underlying craving and tolerance rarely vanish so easily. So your best shot is to abandon the notion of picking and choosing from the good parts of drinking while discarding the downside. They're inseparable. Each sip offers you the same cycle, and your body responds exactly as it's conditioned to do.

My own story was a laundry list of attempts at "bailing out the Titanic with a bucket." I vowed to have a glass of water for every glass of wine. I tried saving the booze for fancy occasions only, only to find that practically everything—birthdays, promotions, random Tuesday promotions—became "fancy" enough. I tried doping myself with prescription medication that punishes you if you drink. The trouble was, if I knew a big party lay ahead, I'd simply skip the pill. That's the entire problem with discipline-based solutions: they assume you'll be rational at your most compromised moments. The same delusions that keep you tethered to drinking end up sabotaging any routine you create.

Remember also that rewiring your brain takes time. You didn't become dependent overnight, so dethroning illusions won't happen in a week. Some people have that sudden eureka moment and never look back, while others read these ideas multiple times before something clicks. Sometimes you step away from the beliefs, then drift back. Every time you catch yourself drifting, that's an opportunity to remember the illusions aren't real. You keep going until clarity is strong enough that alcohol no longer entices you.

It might help to reflect on what a "moderation" plan would look like if it actually worked. Possibly you'd be measuring out an exact number of drinks, or forcing yourself to skip certain days. Notice that all these approaches revolve around forcibly policing your behavior to hamper something you're still convinced is valuable. Doesn't that sound exhausting? Does it truly feel like a permanent fix? If you remain half convinced that a moderate amount of alcohol is wonderful, the craving eventually finds a crack in your fortress. It's the mousetrap scenario again: if the cheese still looks good to you, you'll step forward to nibble. The real epiphany is seeing cheese for what it is—bait with a lethal spring. Once you truly see it, the desire to step on that trap disappears. No complicated routine needed.

A big chunk of success is about letting go of future predictions. If you fixate on never drinking again for your entire life, that can be paralyzing. The mind flips out: "What about birthdays, Christmas, your sister's wedding?" That's a classic tactic of delusions to scare you back to alcohol. Instead, you handle each day, each hour, each scenario as it arises. You say, "Right now, alcohol doesn't benefit me." Then, if you find your mind leaping to next month's stressful event, gently remind yourself that illusions have no clue how you'll feel next month. It's just speculation. The future isn't real. This second is. Right now, do you want alcohol or do you want clarity?

Gradually, as lies crumble and you keep choosing clarity, the habit of alcohol recedes. You might wake up one morning and realize you're not even thinking about alcohol much. That's how you know it worked. You're not sitting around craving with a forced grin. You're just living as though the entire notion of daily alcohol is outdated. If a craving blips up, you see it as something fleeting, not the epic meltdown it once was. You might even smile at how ridiculous the illusions seem from your new vantage point. That's real freedom.

So while moderation might sound appealing, it's usually a coded way of saying, "I want to keep my illusions but reduce the negative consequences." If beliefs remain, the negativity remains, because illusions breed conflict. And it's the conflict that pushes you to keep alcohol in your life. So, ironically, if you truly want freedom, stepping fully out of the mousetrap is far simpler than half-hopping around inside it. Letting it go entirely is the more stable path. Yes, it can feel radical, especially in a culture that glamorizes daily drinking, but radical solutions often match radical illusions. You can't be "a little bit free." You either are or you aren't.

One day, you may look back and find that the idea of "cutting down" was far more complicated and burdensome than simply quitting. When lies are gone, the rest becomes natural. You don't measure drinks or set arbitrary rules. You just don't want alcohol overshadowing your days anymore. That's the quiet, unforced peace that emerges when illusions evaporate. It's not that you're forcibly controlling your drinking—it's that the sedative no longer enthralls you. In that sense, you haven't lost a friend; you've gained a calm you might have thought impossible.

Q7. Is It Too Late For Me To Stop Drinking?

I got an email recently from a woman who'd been drinking dangerously for decades. By her own account, she was broken by it—her daily reality a spiraling loop of shame, guilt, and waking up with that weary, hung-over feeling she thought would never go away. Most heartbreakingly, she concluded her message with, "I want nothing more than to escape this poison, but it might be too late for me now—I'm turning 60 next month."

She expected me to confirm her suspicion, perhaps to say it's futile trying to quit once you reach a certain age. Maybe she imagined that because she'd lost so many years to drinking, a new life was no longer feasible. But I had quite a different perspective, which is that no matter your circumstances, if you still have breath, it's absolutely worth stopping. The delusions might try to convince you otherwise. Let's consider why illusions about "too late" or "better off just continuing" are so misleading.

One misguided premise is that anything beyond a certain age is a write-off. It's as if you turn 60 and lose any chance at improvement. When I was a kid, I saw people over 40 as ancient, but now that I'm well beyond that threshold, life is more joyful than ever. I look back and remember how, in my younger years, I was loaded with rebellion, anger, and selfish impulses. It's only later that you get a calmer, more profound perspective on what truly matters. Alcohol, on the other hand, keeps whispering: "Without me, your future is a grim wasteland." That's one of the illusions that traps people in daily alcohol. If you think about it logically, the suggestion that your best plan is to keep ingesting a depressant for your final decades is wildly irrational. This is a substance that can devastate your finances, health, and relationships. Yet the beliefs run so deep that they become a voice inside your own head, claiming to be your friend.

The question arises: why can't those in the throes of alcoholism simply moderate, especially once they reach a certain age? Often, they have tried. Repeatedly. They vow to have only one glass, only on weekends, only after 5:00 p.m. But eventually, they find themselves overshooting that limit. That's the nature of the condition. Once you cross a threshold of dependence, attempts at moderation turn into an endless test of willpower. And if the lies remain—if part of you still sees alcohol as a benefit—then eventually the seduction proves too strong. If a heroin addict promised to inject only on Tuesdays, would anyone be confident that plan would hold up for an entire year? Of course not. The same dynamic often plays out for problem drinkers. The big difference is that our culture sees heroin as taboo, while daily wine or beer is labeled normal. This labeling difference changes nothing about the fundamental trap.

Imagine seeing a sinkhole in your backyard. You can't fix it by tossing in a few shovel loads of dirt, hoping partial filling will do. If the underlying structure is compromised, eventually it reopens. Moderating a serious drinking problem is a bit like that. You think you've contained the sinkhole, but illusions remain about the "harmless enjoyment" of alcohol. Over time, your mind starts rationalizing larger and larger amounts. Alcohol is cunning in that regard, luring you with the idea that the final outcome will be different this time—maybe just two drinks a night, strictly measured. But each day ends up turning "strictly measured" into "just a bit more." You've probably experimented with multiple such routines—maybe you resolved to skip spirits and only drink beer, or to keep a bottle in a locked cabinet, or to insert a forced break by going dry for a few weeks each year. In the end, these short-term strategies unravel because they never uproot the illusions themselves. The delusions that alcohol is beneficial or essential remain untouched, so the ground is still unstable.

Back to that woman about to turn 60, who was worried she'd missed her chance: the simple act of stopping, even now, might yield more physical repair than she imagines. The liver is resilient. If you quit before genuine end-stage damage sets in, your body can regenerate and reclaim lost ground. Of course, if you're extremely far gone, you may face irreversible complications. But for anyone not on death's doorstep, there's genuine hope. Even if you only lived another five or ten years, would you rather spend them feeling anchored by alcohol and gloom, or would you choose vitality and presence? It's revealing how delusions can twist logic: they warn that it's "too late," so you might as well keep drinking. Meanwhile, your body begs for a respite from constant toxicity. Alcohol is notoriously unhelpful for "late-stage" anything. It doesn't matter if you're 22 or 92, alcohol doesn't cure a single ailment. The illusions imply that alcohol is a coping mechanism for life's challenges. Actually, alcohol is just alcohol. The problems remain.

I sometimes bring up a cruel quip that "alcohol is a depressant." But I see it more as a negative amplifier. If life is going well—dancing and laughing with friends—alcohol can appear to enhance the mood. But the opposite is also true: if you're sad and stuck, daily alcohol sinks you deeper into the pit. People who are physically dependent on the substance reach a point where it no longer elevates them—it drags them down as though strapped to an anchor. So the illusions that once promised excitement or relaxation start fueling heartbreak and despair, especially if the person can't moderate, yet keeps trying. The emotional whiplash is profound. Mornings become repeated guilt sessions, nights become alcohol marathons, and the middle hours revolve around "maintenance" to avoid withdrawal. That's not exactly living. So the question "Is it too late?" might be better framed as "Do you still want to salvage your life, or do you prefer to let alcohol overshadow any remaining joys?"

In truth, our programming can and does get dismantled. You see alcohol for what it is: a slow-acting chemical that impersonates a friend but systematically steals your time, money, self-esteem, and mental clarity. Once you see that, you can't unsee it. By that point, daily alcohol is about as appealing as daily spoonfuls of bleach. So to answer the question about whether it's too late at 60: absolutely not. This minute is brand new. One can't know how many days remain, but you can choose not to let beliefs devour the ones you do have. Maybe you have only a few more years—wouldn't you rather greet them as a sober, awake version of yourself? Or perhaps you have decades left. In that case, why hand so many more years to a mind-numbing routine that's proven to deliver zero genuine good?

Incidentally, you can't moderate illusions away, either. They must be faced. If your illusions revolve around "Alcohol is my last pleasure, and life is dismal without it," cutting down is simply a slower route to the same lies. You're rationing the sedative, never addressing the root cause. I've known people who say, "I only drink on special occasions," but then declare half the year's calendar as special. The illusions find a way to expand. The entire concept is built on the false premise that alcohol is somehow beneficial in small doses, which is exactly the problem in the first place.

Even from a purely medical standpoint, the liver is known to have remarkable regenerative capacity. Stopping at 60, 70, or 80 can still yield improvements in your markers, your energy, your mood. It's a cliche to say "Better late than never," but it's also undeniably accurate. This is your life, not a mere runthrough. Whether you're done with alcohol at 30 or at 65, from the next day forward, you get to enjoy mornings with a clear head, nights with restful sleep, and a conscience free of daily regrets. That's a gift worth pursuing, delusions be damned.

Some worry that life might be sad without alcohol. But is alcohol truly the great antidote to sadness? My experience says otherwise. Drinking rarely solves sorrow or heartbreak.

It dulls you for a few hours, then you wake up to the same heartbreak plus a headache. Meanwhile, you've lost precious time. If your illusions told you alcohol was your only friend in later life, I'd argue that's a friend that whispers destructive lies in your ear. "It's too late, you can't change, nobody cares." That's no friend. Why cling to it?

Over and over, beliefs revolve around fear. Fear that you can't handle emotional pain or boredom without alcohol. Fear that you're not fun or interesting enough if you aren't half-buzzed. Fear that you've used up your prime years, so who cares what you do with the rest. Yet if you systematically question them, none stand up to scrutiny. You can find better ways to handle emotions, connect with people, or bring excitement to your days. Drinking is never the only option. It just dresses up as an easy fix. It's a costume party that eventually ends, leaving you stranded on the sofa at 3 a.m. with a big cleanup job.

In the end, illusions fade the moment you see them in the daylight. The 60-year-old who wrote me realized, after some reflection, that she'd already wasted enough precious time being knocked out on her couch, missing real experiences with family and friends. She decided she wanted to live her next decade or two feeling alive instead of numb. By her next birthday, she was free. She told me she only regretted not quitting sooner, but I reminded her that regrets accomplish nothing. The important part is she found clarity now, in the present second. If there's a moral to her story, it's that illusions about "too late" or "only enjoy in moderation" often melt away once you accept that alcohol has no true advantage.

So if a voice inside your head says you're past the point of no return, note that it's lies talking. If you're reading these words, you're still breathing, and that means you can still choose. The delusions hold no real power the moment you realize they're illusions. That's your opportunity to step off the trap once and for all, no matter what your birth certificate says. The best day to quit was yesterday. The second best day is this one right here.

Putting it all together: you might have some lingering questions that aren't addressed here. That's normal. Everyone's journey from alcohol to clarity is personal. The beliefs around alcohol can show up in dozens of ways, from your big holiday gatherings to your weekly social rituals. The bottom line is that if you've recognized that the illusions are just illusions, the best path forward is to eliminate the substance altogether. Shortcuts like "milk thistle" or "cut down so my friends don't tease me" are half-measures that keep lies alive.

Is it easy? Not always. You'll face the odd meltdown from your old drinking buddies who can't imagine an identity outside the bar stool. You might have surreal dreams for a while. You might yearn for a quick fix on big social occasions. But those challenges are part of the process, and each time you face one, you strengthen your conviction. The illusions that once painted alcohol as essential slowly crumble. Eventually, you find yourself observing drunk people at a party and marveling that you ever found that scene appealing.

If you find yourself searching for further reassurance or suspecting you're alone in your experiences, trust me, countless others have passed the same mile markers. The path may twist, but it leads to a place where you're free from alcohol, illusions, and hangovers. And each time you read a question from someone else worried about Christmas dinners or protective herbs, you can't help but grin at how universal these delusions are. They're precisely the cunning lies that keep society enthralled by an otherwise unremarkable depressant. But once you see them for what they are, there's simply no going back. And that, my friend, is the best kind of no-return scenario.

Chapter 17: The Complete Solution

I often compare alcohol addiction to stumbling into quicksand. In both cases, you underestimate the danger and carry on until you're suddenly in deep trouble. People who wander into a patch of real quicksand usually only realize the peril once they're sinking past their waist, at which point they're struggling, gasping, and flailing. Alcohol is no different: you only recognize the extent of the risk once you're already half-submerged.

It might help to imagine what happens in a region prone to quicksand. You rarely see warning signs smack in the middle of it; they're posted far in advance, on the perimeter, telling you that continuing forward is unwise. That's exactly how it should be with alcohol. Think back to the very first sip of booze you tried. Chances are, your first reaction was sheer distaste—maybe you even retched a bit. That recoil should have been the giant neon sign: "Danger—turn back." Yet we rarely see it that way, because we glance around and notice everyone else appears to be enjoying their drinks, sipping away as though it's the most pleasurable thing on Earth. And so we persist, telling ourselves we'll learn to like it if we keep practicing.

In reality, that vow to "keep practicing" is the moment we choose to walk closer to the center of the bog, ignoring the warning signs that drinking foul-tasting poison might not be the best plan. Eventually, we sense we're stuck. Like a person stuck in quicksand, we start panicking, thrashing around, struggling to escape. But that's the nature of quicksand: the more aggressively you flail, the faster you sink. It's an unwinnable fight if you rely on frantic force. Trying to use sheer willpower to manage or reduce your drinking without changing your perspective on the drug is akin to thrashing wildly in that pit. Every time you fail to moderate, you sink deeper into shame and stress. Then you feel a stronger urge to drink again because, of course, you see alcohol as your stress reliever. It's a lethal loop.

Like quicksand, it's pretty rare to get out on your own. Generally, you need someone reaching out a helpful hand, someone who can coach you on the steps to take—and perhaps more importantly, the steps not to take. That's one reason I wrote this book. There are so many successful, intelligent people who live with a secret: they're on the verge of losing control with alcohol, but they're too afraid to seek help. Others keep telling themselves, "I'll handle it," until the crisis is undeniable. By then, they've possibly lost a job or a relationship, or their health is in shambles. The alternative is to let someone show you the safe way back to solid ground before the downward spiral grows too strong.

Reading this book is a decisive first step. Just by investing your time and money here, you've admitted a potential problem that many remain in denial about for years or decades. If, however, you're a high-performing individual who has much to lose—like a stable career, a strong reputation, a loving family—then ignoring the help that's offered is risky. I often ask people to consider what their life might look like in five or ten years if they simply continued the same drinking pattern, or worse, if it escalates to match their rising tolerance. That's a grim forecast, one that can impact your income, your social standing, and your closest relationships.

Helping problem drinkers is a passion for me, and it's essentially all I do these days. If you join me at a live quit drinking event, you'll see me throw everything I have into the cause of turning beliefs around. I suspect it might surprise you to see how many folks in the room share your story: outwardly successful, yet quietly drowning in booze at night. Every year, I also work privately with a handful of clients, practically serving as their personal sponsor. We speak regularly, keep close tabs on progress, and ensure they nail this problem once and for all. That's how much I believe in this mission. I know for a fact that a lot of conventional tactics (like going cold turkey with nothing but willpower) simply lead to exhaustion and repeated failure.

And I prefer to avoid letting people waste more of their precious time. My approach is all about addressing the illusions that keep you in that bog, so you can stand on solid ground without feeling deprived.

There's a reason I call it the most effective alcohol cessation solution around today, and it's not just hype. We connect on multiple layers, from personal mentorship calls to hypnosis to a step-by-step video course. There's a secret online group where participants find a supportive, non-judgmental community of peers. You're never judged; you're simply supported. Add 75 hours of coaching, 90 days of intensive follow-up, and lifetime support for extra reassurance, and you have something more akin to a well-structured rescue plan than a typical self-help program. Even so, I'd say the single biggest factor remains your readiness to accept that extended hand.

Returning to the quicksand metaphor: if you found someone trapped waist-deep, arms flailing, you wouldn't just watch them. You'd either throw them a rope or get a branch to help them out. If they were to say, "Nah, I'm just going to keep thrashing until I get out on my own," you'd be baffled. You know it doesn't work that way. Yet so many of us do exactly that with alcohol—insisting we'll handle it alone, even as we sink deeper.

Part of the reason we cling to illusions of self-reliance is that society normalizes heavy drinking. You likely have a friend group or a professional circle where it's almost a badge of honor to "man up" or "woman up" and match everyone drink for drink. But that's the same social compulsion that leads us astray in the first place. Just because an entire crowd is walking into the quicksand doesn't make it any less deadly. That's a crucial realization. Popular does not equal safe or smart—plenty of historical practices once deemed normal have turned out to be disastrous.

So how do we pivot from lies to acceptance, from panic to rescue? We start by confronting the simple fact that the months or years we've spent building tolerance and ignoring warning signs haven't solved anything. It might have delayed the meltdown, but at what cost? Quicksand doesn't grant you a special pass for bravado. Alcohol doesn't grant you an immunity from heartbreak or liver damage just because you've learned to drink steadily without slurring in front of your boss. Over time, it catches up with you, physically and mentally.

That's where a helping hand comes into play—someone who's seen all the illusions, walked out of them, and guided others down the same path. My approach is about unmasking illusions so thoroughly that you stop wanting alcohol entirely. The idea isn't to forcibly abstain, bracing each day in a white-knuckle stance, but rather to see the truth so clearly that alcohol no longer appeals. Once you get to that point, you don't need rules about limiting yourself to weekends or only drinking two glasses. It doesn't cross your mind to drink more than zero, because you see no upside in a mild anesthetic that drains your wallet, your health, and your clarity.

Although the notion of quitting might still sound a bit scary, my clients typically discover that once illusions dissolve, the fear dissolves, too. Fear comes from believing you're losing something precious. If I told you to give up drinking bleach, you'd laugh—obviously, that's no sacrifice. Soon, that's how you view alcohol. At that point, your quicksand problem is resolved, and you don't need daily willpower to remain free. You're simply disinterested in sinking again.

Of course, I'm not oblivious to the social dimension. You might worry how coworkers will react if you politely decline after-work rounds at the pub. Or how family gatherings might shift if you're the only one not filling your glass. But the alternative—keeping up appearances while you sink deeper—just isn't worth it. You might adopt short-term strategies, like making your own non-alcoholic beverage or leaving earlier than usual if things get rowdy. Over time, your acquaintances adapt. Those who can't handle your new stance might drift away, which can sting initially. Yet in the long run, you form new connections with people who respect your choices. That's an upgrade.

So if you're at the point of asking yourself, "What next?" or "How do I ensure I don't slip back once the panic is gone?" the answer is straightforward. Accept the hand offered. Take the plan or program that resonates with you. Go all in. If that means daily mentorship calls, hypnosis, or an online forum to keep you accountable, don't be embarrassed or hesitant. You have a lot more to lose by clinging to beliefs than you do by letting someone guide you out. It's astonishing how quickly you can reclaim your life when you feel the ground under your feet again.

The gambler's mindset can be persuasive, especially if you're used to success in other fields. Maybe you're telling yourself, "I've been fine this long; I'll figure this out if it becomes critical." But that's gambler talk. The stakes are high right now—your job, your marriage, your relationship with your children, your future health. Why gamble with a guaranteed losing bet when a guaranteed exit path is right in front of you?

When you do accept that help, it's like letting someone anchor a rope around you. They instruct you to stop flailing and instead follow a calm set of steps. You realize your own hectic thrashing was half of why you couldn't pull yourself up. Similarly, with alcohol, the illusions that keep you spinning your wheels—"I need it to relax," "I can't go a day without it," "it's not that bad yet"—are the mental equivalent of frantic limbs in the quicksand. Stop letting them run the show, and let logic, guidance, and clarity take over.

And that's precisely the purpose of the support system I provide. Some read this book and find that alone is enough to spark their transformation. Others feel they need the personalized approach—someone on the phone, someone who knows the territory intimately, who can say, "I see you; I've been there; here's your best move." Whatever form the hand takes, the key is being willing to grab it. There's no shame in acknowledging you're stuck. The real shame would be continuing to sink out of pride.

As you stand at this crossroads, imagine yourself in another year if nothing changes. Picture that future: same illusions, maybe a bigger tolerance, possibly some new complications with your partner, your boss, or your own mental health. Compare that to a future where you take a bold step, accept help, and watch lies crumble. The second scenario might feel oddly daunting—after all, you're used to alcohol. But it's more likely to result in genuine contentment, more energy, and deeper self-respect than you've felt in years.

Given that choice, the wise person knows it's better to step out of the quicksand. Once you're free, you see just how claustrophobic and draining it was to be trapped. Ultimately, you realize it doesn't even matter that the rest of the world believes quicksand is cozy. You know the truth now, and nobody can talk you back in.

If you still feel you need more help and support to begin and succeed at this journey, the next step is to spend an hour with me in a free quit drinking webinar, I will explain the process in detail and make taking the first step easy, reserve your place at: www.stopdrinkingexpert.com

Craig Beck

Recommended links
• https://www.CraigBeck.com
• https://www.StopDrinkingExpert.com

Follow Craig Beck on Social Media
• Facebook: https://www.facebook.com/craigbeckbooks

- X: http://twitter.com/CraigBeck

You Don't Have to Do It Alone…
Join the online coaching club that has helped over 250,000 people like you regain control of their drinking.

Online Course

Break Free from Alcohol Instantly – No Willpower, No Meetings, No Costly Rehab!

Join 250,000+ Who've Transformed Their Lives with This Proven Method! FREE How To Stop Drinking Webinar and eBook

www.stopdrinkingexpert.com

Are you sick and tired of feeling sick and tired?

Maybe you are finding that more and more you are turning to alcohol on an evening to 'relax' and cope with life?

Perhaps you are dealing with serious health problems, financial worries and failing relationships. Plus the guilt of not giving the people you love the 'real you' anymore?

I understand how you feel!

First of all, you should know that I was a heavy drinker myself. Alcohol became something that I couldn't control despite how miserable it was making me.

I had an outstanding career, beautiful home and family but one by one alcoholism was destroying them all.

Every day I made excuses about why I 'needed' to drink.

All the time, failing to make the connection that my alcoholism was the reason for the vast majority of my problems.

- My health was going downhill fast
- My marriage was falling apart
- I was missing quality time with my children
- My career was going nowhere fast
- I was descending deeper and deeper into debt
- Depression, worry and unhappiness were my life

My drinking was hurting everyone I loved.

My family was everything to me! I would have defended and protected them with my life.

In contrast here I was, badly hurting them myself!

My nightly drinking had turned me into a fat, selfish zombie. I wasn't interested in anything but drinking.

It made me so selfish! As a result I wouldn't go anywhere or do anything unless I could drink at the same time. All clear signs of addiction but still I refused to accept it.

I am ashamed to admit I was a terrible husband and nowhere near the father I set out to be.

There was no way I was going to AA!

I wanted someone to show me how to stop drinking alcohol, but Alcoholics Anonymous was too depressing, also I had my professional reputation to think about. Consequently, I didn't want to stand up in a room full of strangers and label myself 'an alcoholic'.

Rehab was too expensive and I couldn't risk taking an extended leave from work!

I tried almost everything.

From silly gimmicks, herbal supplements and hypnosis through to prescription medication (recklessly ordered from abroad online). It seemed like nothing made any real difference.

This solution' Has Helped Over 250,000 Drinkers

How to stop drinking without all the usual struggle:
When I gave up trying to force myself to cut back. It was only then I discovered how to deal with my alcoholism in a more logical and simple way.

I changed the meaning of alcohol, it stopped being something a saw as a special treat. As a result it became something I saw as nothing more than 'attractively packaged poison'.

Finally, life suddenly became... peaceful, happy and secure.

I lost weight, slept like a baby, reconnected with my family, regained my career and even more.

It became so easy that the years I had struggled to force myself to cut back seemed silly.
I had tried hundreds of times to moderate my drinking. All the time dreaming of drinking like a 'normal' person.

Creating silly rules for myself:

- I told myself I would only drink beer, never wine (FAILED)
- Then I promised I would only drink on special occasions (FAILED)

- I said I would quit drinking at home and only drink socially (FAILED)
- Yet, In all other areas of my life I was successful.

Nobody outside my close family had any idea I was knocking back two bottles of wine a night, every night.

My friends just thought I could 'handle my drink', like it was something to be proud of!

Then I Had A Lightbulb Moment!

Everyone claims that quitting drinking is difficult, miserable and painful right?

The reason is because drinkers the world over are using the same broken 'solution' over and over and expecting the outcome to change.

Trying to force yourself to moderate your drinking has a 95% chance of failure.

So why then does EVERY traditional way of dealing with alcohol addiction still uses this as the 'go to solution'?

Perhaps willpower does not work?

Twelve-step programs tell you that you are broken and always will be

Consequently, you must spend the rest of your life forcing yourself to stay away from the thing you want the most!

Likewise, rehab costs tens of thousands of dollars to do exactly the same thing.

Using prescription medication to deal with any addiction still requires willpower in order to keep taking the tablets.

Plus they come with side-effects worse than a hangover!

Absolutely no judgment or embarrassment - Deal with this entirely in the privacy of your own home.

If it wasn't killing over three million people every year (according to World Health Organization figures) it might even be funny.

But for those of us trapped in the loop, it's not funny. It's a miserable experience.

Therefore, these days I devote my time to showing people how to stop drinking alcohol in a rather more simple way. No embarrassing group meetings, no expensive rehab, no dangerous medications and absolutely zero ineffective willpower.

Your health is going to get dramatically better
Within 3 months of quitting drinking my high blood pressure vanished. More than that, it return to perfectly normal levels, despite being elevated for over a decade.

My sleep apnea cleared up and the scary pain in my side went away and never came back. Therefore, proving to me once and for all that it was being caused by my drinking all along.

Who knows what would have happened if I had carried on drinking.

I lost 57lbs of body fat without any real effort. It turns out there is a lot of calories in all that alcohol I was knocking back.

But my story is not unique. You are about to find out for yourself the significant health benefits of kicking the attractively packaged poison out of your life:

1. Better quality sleep.

2. More energy.
3. Clarity and less brain fog.
4. Clearer skin.
5. Increased mental focus.
6. Effortless weight loss.
7. Improved blood pressure.
8. Reduced risk of cancer.
9. Better immune system.
10. Improved memory function.

Your relationships will get so much better
If you are a problem drinker your relationships are under an unbearable amount of pressure.

The hard truth is, drinkers are focused on when they can have their next drink. As a result they don't spend a lot of time considering how they can be a loving, caring and passionate husband or wife.

When you learn how to stop drinking alcohol using my method, so many good things happen to your relationships:

1. No more drunken arguments and saying things you will regret.
2. More quality time together.
3. Never choosing alcohol over your partner again.
4. Sexual dysfunction and impotence can improve.
5. More passionate and enjoyable sex where you are both 100% present.
6. Stop giving your partner the 'lazy zombie' version of the person they met.
7. Be the loving, attentive parent that you set out to be.
8. Rediscover the authentic you.

Plus: The average member saves thousands... every year

The average member saves over $6000 per year. But alcohol is stealing so much more than the financial cost!

When you're sober, you naturally operate at your maximum capacity. You're lucid, focused, and you wake up feeling like a million bucks every day (this benefit cannot be overstated).

When I was drinking, my effectiveness on any given day might have been around 80%.

Now, I feel like I'm constantly operating at 98% or more. What's incredible is that this improvement has had an exponential impact on the tangible success I've achieved.

Get back in control of your life easily with this course

I always dreamed of escaping the rat race and being my own boss. For over a decade my drinking problem prevented me from even getting started.

As soon as I discovered how to stop drinking alcohol for good, my life started to change in the most amazing ways.

I quit drinking and then I quit my miserable 9 to 5 job. Today, I never go to 'the office', likewise, I am never stuck in the dreaded commute and I don't have a boss to answer to.

Thousands of people just like you have done exactly the same thing with my help...

Just as soon as they kick this life limiting poison out of their lives for good.

Decide now & be the next to quit drinking without any of the usual hard work or struggle.

Sign up for my next free quit drinking webinar and I will personally take you through the easy, step by step process:

www.stopdrinkingexpert.com

Printed in Dunstable, United Kingdom